Public Child Welfare

Public Child Welfare

A CASEBOOK FOR LEARNING AND TEACHING

Sarah Carnochan, Lisa Molinar, Joanne Brown,
Lisa Botzler, Karen Gunderson, Colleen
Henry, and Michael J. Austin

 cognella® | ACADEMIC PUBLISHING

Bassim Hamadeh, CEO and Publisher
Kassie Graves, Vice President of Editorial
Amy Smith, Project Editor
Abbey Hastings, Associate Production Editor
Jess Estrella, Senior Graphic Designer
Sara Schennum, Licensing Associate
Don Kesner, Interior Designer
Natalie Piccotti, Senior Marketing Manager
Jamie Giganti, Director of Academic Publishing

The case plan objectives are excerpted from the client case records in California's Child Welfare Services/Case Management System, overseen by the California Department of Social Services.

Cover image copyright © 2018 iStockphoto LP/Beastfromeast.

Printed in the United States of America.

ISBN: 978-1-5165-3682-5 (pbk) / 978-1-5165-3683-2 (br)

Brief Contents

Detailed Contents

Chapter 17: Ronald R. 129

Ronald R. is a 10-year-old boy adopted out of foster care, raised with another adoptive boy who became increasingly out of control as they reached pre-teen years

Chapter 18: Sophia W. 135

Sophia W. is a 10-year-old girl abused in a "power struggle" with mother with mental health issues; placement with father was not supported initially, but succeeded

Chapter 19: Nathan D. 145

Nathan D. is a seven-year-old boy who was injured by his mother while his parents were fighting, resulting in their arrest; legal guardianship with grandparents recommended

Preface

In our 20 plus years of a research partnership with county human service agencies and their child welfare divisions, we have witnessed the commitment, compassion, and skill that child welfare workers bring to the complexities involved in engaging and supporting children and their families. Yet, child welfare research typically focuses on the problems and challenges faced by child welfare systems. While examining these issues is important in order to identify areas where services and outcomes need to be improved, our research describes, in part, the everyday stories of the workers and families involved in child welfare services that include both successes and sorrows.

Amidst a continuing avalanche of new policy directives and practice initiatives, social workers must navigate the urgent and intersecting needs of children and families, making decisions that will affect the lives and outcomes of the people they serve. Child welfare workers need to understand the challenges and opportunities in this field of practice. The detailed, rich descriptions of the cases in this casebook capture the complex, messy, challenging work that child welfare workers engage in every day. In addition to the evidence that can be generated by research, these cases provide additional opportunities to learn from practice wisdom.

The cases are derived from five years of data-mining research drawing on public child welfare case records that document the complexity and trajectory of each case. As mandatory automated client data systems have evolved, the scope and level of detail documented in case records has expanded, along with the documentation demands placed on social workers. By developing these cases, we honor both the practice and the documentation involved in child welfare services.

Our student research assistants alerted us to the significant learning they gained from coding and synthesizing these case records. Rarely are such complex cases accessible for use in instructional settings. As a result, this casebook of real-life cases is one of the few resources in the human services that feature the presentation of complex child welfare cases for the purpose of pre-service and in-service education.

OVERVIEW OF THE CASEBOOK

The casebook is appropriate for multiple settings and with diverse learner groups, including social work practice courses, child welfare fieldwork seminars, and agency-based training programs. The casebook can be used in a capstone course at the end of the MSW program to provide cases for use in applying and integrating classroom and field-based learning experiences. It could also be used in agency-based induction training of new child welfare workers. Agency-based supervisors can use the casebook as a mentoring tool in their efforts to expand the critical thinking skills of staff members. Nonprofit child welfare agencies under contract with state and local governments will also find the casebook to be a useful training tool.

The major components of the casebook include 1) twenty cases from four California county child welfare agencies; 2) an introductory chapter that provides a context for understanding the cases in relationship to relevant national and state policy and practice; and 3) a case overview chapter that explains how the cases were created, examines the relationship between case documentation and child welfare practice, and acknowledges the challenges that difficult case material may pose for some learners.

The Cases

Students and practitioners engaged in the case analysis process will be able to demonstrate their critical thinking skills, acquire a wider understanding of the range of real-life practice issues in public child welfare, use the cases to demonstrate end-of-program competencies in both case analysis and service planning, and use the casebook to demonstrate their practice competencies and understanding in end-of-program job interviews. The cases can equip them to expand their knowledge of public child welfare client needs and resources, effectively engage in case conferences as well as case record reviews as part of an agency's program of continuous quality improvement of services, and identify and manage the difficult emotional responses that can arise in response to the experiences of children and families involved in child welfare services.

One of the unique benefits offered by these real cases is the documentation of the unfolding of a case over time. It is immensely time-consuming to review and summarize an entire set of records associated with a child welfare case. Consequently, students and new workers rarely, if ever, have the opportunity to review an entire case, constraining their ability to anticipate long-term effects of their judgments and actions. The cases also enable students and workers to learn from cases that do not lead to good results for children or parents, as well as those where the desired outcomes are achieved. Learners will also be confronted with the need to make sense of a case based on documentation that may be incomplete or unclear, contains inconsistencies, or is difficult to interpret, providing "real-life" exposure to cases documented by multiple caseworkers.

Introductory Chapter

The introductory chapter frames the cases within the context of relevant national and state policy and practice. As a result, the chapter enables instructors and learners to make the connection between policy and practice guidelines and how these are or are not implemented at the direct service level. In conjunction with the Discussion

Questions at the end of each chapter, the initial chapter can guide analysis that contrasts and compares these California-based cases with jurisdictions in other states.

Case Overview Chapter

Chapter 2 explains how the cases were created. It examines the relationship between case documentation and child welfare practice, and it highlights the challenges related to documentation in child welfare. It concludes with an acknowledgement that some learners may find that this material poses emotional challenges and provides suggestions for how to address these challenges and difficulties if they arise.

SPECIAL FEATURES

The casebook includes several useful aids to support teaching and learning, including discussion questions, instructor materials related to case-based learning, a matrix of case elements that summarizes client and service characteristics across the cases, and a glossary.

Discussion Questions

Each case is accompanied by a series of discussion questions designed to structure and guide critical reflection by students. Developed by child welfare experts with extensive experience as administrators and trainers, these questions can be used to help learners identify and articulate their own perceptions and opinions, analyze decision-making in the case, and develop their own judgments related to service delivery. For example, questions related to Chapter 8 include the following: 1) If Shawna had been placed in the custody of the child welfare agency at birth, how might her case have differed with respect to her placement, visitation, and her mother's case plan? 2) How does it complicate cases when the parent is a current dependent? 3) What could Shawna's social worker have done differently to involve Shawna's father? 4) Would Shawna's mother be considered a commercially sexually exploited child or a prostitute? Explain your answer (see p. 66).

Case-Based Teaching and Learning

Materials designed to support instructors in case-based teaching and learning are provided in Appendix A. This information draws on the years of teaching using case-based teaching methods on the part of one of the co-authors, as well as related scholarly literature. The materials provide concrete examples and suggestions designed to help instructors and learners prepare themselves for the effective use of the casebook. For example, the Appendix contains a section on strategies for mapping the local child welfare policy and practice context, with recommendations that include 1) searching the website(s) of the state and/or county social service agencies to identify relevant policies, initiatives, and practice guidelines; 2) identifying any risk and safety assessment instruments used by child welfare agencies to inform decision-making; and 3) reviewing the state's or county's System Improvement Plan developed for the Federal Child and Family Services Review (see p. 178).

Matrix of Case Elements

The matrix of case elements displays an array of key service characteristics and case characteristics associated with each case. These provide a visual overview of the diversity of the cases, as well as the complex and intersecting needs and events that families and children experience. The matrix can also be used as a tool to identify cases that feature specific issues that an instructor wants to examine with learners. For example, an instructor who seeks to use cases that involve commercially sexually exploited children would be able to use the matrix to identify the relevant cases of Tina C. (Chapter 4), Shawna L. (Chapter 8), and Jayden M. (Chapter 11) (see p. 185).

Glossary

The juvenile dependency system and court process are governed by federal and state laws and regulations that set forth procedural requirements and outline the rights and responsibilities of the parties involved. Child welfare case records contain numerous references to these legal and bureaucratic aspects of the dependency system that can be difficult to interpret for those who are new to the child welfare field. The records also contain acronyms and jargon that are based in the local practice and policy context. The Glossary provides definitions and explanations for these terms and includes references to online sources where interested readers can find additional information. For example, it includes the following explanation of LiveScan and accompanying link to a fact sheet on the California Department of Social Services website (see pp. 213–232):

> LiveScan: Background checks for caregivers require fingerprinting in California; LiveScan refers to the electronic fingerprinting technology that is used. Adapted from http://www.cdss.ca.gov/inforesources/Community-Care/Caregiver-Background-Check/LiveScan

ACKNOWLEDGMENTS

This casebook reflects the dedication and efforts of many individuals. We want to acknowledge the valuable contributions of the directors, managers, and staff of the child welfare agencies that participated in the studies and provided the foundation for the cases. We would also like to acknowledge the commitment and hard work of research assistants, including MSW students, doctoral students, and post-doctoral fellows who played a critical role in extracting and coding the case record data.

Thanks also go to the reviewers who provided valuable comments that strengthened the manuscript: Stacy Bishop (Saginaw Valley State University), Kathy LaPlante (University of South Dakota), Adrienne Pollichemi (La Salle University, Philadelphia), and Terry Shaw (University of Maryland).

The casebook was developed with financial support from the Bay Area Social Services Consortium (California) and the Mack Center on Nonprofit and Public Sector Management in the Human Services, School of Social Welfare, University of California, Berkeley.

Introduction to Public Child Welfare Practice and Policy Context

1

BACKGROUND

C hild welfare is an area of social work practice that focuses on responding to complex family dynamics and trauma. Child welfare services involve involuntary clients and are overseen by court systems that operate with due process rights and legal representation for children and parents. It is a field impacted by federal and state mandates, complicated funding structures, legal consent decrees, and advocates representing diverse interests. The intersection of these conflicting and colliding forces creates complex practice challenges for child welfare workers as they work to ensure child safety, reunify families, and where reunification is not achieved, provide children with permanency.

The aim of this casebook is to foster clarity and understanding about the work being done in the field, as well as the broader policy issues that generate public debate about the role of government involvement in the welfare of children. Child welfare practice is documented in case records created by child welfare workers that form the basis for these Teaching and Learning Cases. These real-life cases provide the foundation for engaging in a case-based learning process that involves dissecting decisions made in actual cases and analyzing how different interventions impact outcomes with children, parents, and families. Case-based learning can strengthen understanding and skills among child welfare practitioners, enabling successful engagement in child welfare practice as well as with the federal case review process known as the Child and Family Services Review (CFSR) and state Continuous Quality Improvement (CQI) systems.

This chapter provides an overview of the national and state policy frameworks and practice guidelines that shape child welfare practice at the local level.

NATIONAL CHILD WELFARE CONTEXT: ACCOUNTABILITY AND SYSTEM IMPROVEMENT

On November 19, 1997, President Bill Clinton signed the Adoption and Safe Families Act (ASFA) into law. ASFA was the culmination of two decades of advocacy and research about the growing numbers of children in foster care. ASFA established national goals and standards for child protection and established timely permanency as a metric of child welfare practice. The orientation of the public responsibility for children removed from their parents due to abuse and neglect shifted from being primarily delegated to the social work arena to a system overseen by the courts, with attorneys appointed to represent parents, children, and the child protection agency. In addition, ASFA mandated that the federal Children's Bureau work with state and local child welfare officials and advocates to develop outcome measures to assess states' performance in operating child protection and child welfare systems. Through the newly instituted CFSR, funding for child welfare was tied to compliance with federal regulations to ensure that states provided the data needed for assessment and measurement (Spar & Shuman, 2004).

The CFSR process is designed to assess and monitor each state's performance with respect to their conformity with specific outcomes related to child safety, permanency, and well-being for children and families. The reviews depended on in-depth analysis of randomly selected cases, stakeholder interviews, and systematically collected data in each state. Since the enactment of the federal legislation, two rounds of reviews have been completed and the third round began in 2016. No state was able to demonstrate substantial conformity in the initial rounds, and, as a result, Program Improvement Plans were required for all states (Children's Bureau, 2015). The most recent round of CFSR reviews reflects an overall shift away from complying with checklists that focused on process and toward an emphasis on practice with children and families to achieve 1) the desired outcomes, 2) engagement with the practitioners and stakeholders, and 3) the use of quantitative data indicators to improve decision-making.

CFSR Outcomes and Data Indicators

Within the three broad outcome domains of safety, permanency, and well-being that frame the CFSR process, there are seven corresponding data indicators related to safety and permanency, as well as seven systemic factors (King, Needell, Dawson, Webster, & Magruder, 2015). The safety and permanency outcomes and indicators include the following:

Safety Outcomes

a. Children are, first and foremost, protected from abuse and neglect.

1. Data Indicator: Maltreatment recurrence. Of all children who were victims of a substantiated or indicated report of maltreatment during a 12-month reporting period, what percent were victims of another substantiated or indicated maltreatment allegation within 12 months of their initial report?

2. Data Indicator: Maltreatment in foster care. Of all children in foster care during a 12-month period, what is the rate of victimization per day of foster care (79 FR 61241, 2014)?

b. Children are safely maintained in their homes whenever possible and appropriate (Children's Bureau, 2015).

Permanency Outcomes

a. Children have permanency and stability in their living situations.

1. Data Indicator: Permanency within 12 months of entry for 12-month entry cohort. Of all children who enter foster care in a 12-month period, what percent discharged to permanency within 12 months of entering foster care?

2. Data Indicator: Permanency in 12 months for children in care 12–23 months. Of all children in foster care on the first day of a 12-month period who had been in foster care (in that episode) between 12 and 23 months, what percent discharged from foster care to permanency within 12 months of the first day of the 12-month period?

3. Data Indicator: Permanency in 12 months for children in care 24 months or more. Of all children in foster care on the first day of a 12-month period who had been in foster care (in that episode) for 24 months or more, what percent discharged to permanency within 12 months of the first day of the 12-month period?

4. Data Indicator: Placement stability. Of all children who enter foster care in a 12-month period, what is the rate of placement moves per day of foster care?

5. Data Indicator: Re-entry to care in 12 months. Of all children who enter foster care in a 12-month period who discharged within 12 months to reunification, living with a relative(s), or guardianship, what percent re-enter foster care within 12 months of their discharge (79 FR 61241, 2014)?

b. The continuity of family relationships and connections is preserved for families (Children's Bureau, 2015).

Family and Child Well-Being Outcomes
    a.   Families have enhanced capacity to provide for their children's needs.
    b.   Children receive appropriate services to meet their educational needs.
    c.   Children receive adequate services to meet their physical and mental health needs (Children's Bureau, 2015).

Systemic Factors
The reviews also involve evaluation of state performance with respect to seven systemic factors. This component of the review process focuses on compliance with specific federal requirements for child welfare systems, as well as the effectiveness of the system, by assessing 1) the statewide child welfare information system; 2) the case review system; 3) the quality assurance system; 4) staff and provider training; 5) the service array and resource development; 6) the agency's responsiveness to the community; and 7) foster and adoptive parent licensing, recruitment, and retention (Children's Bureau, 2015; King et al., 2015).

Continuous Quality Improvement (CQI)

On August 27, 2012, the federal Administration for Children and Families (ACF) called for strengthening the quality assurance (QA) processes of all states through the CQI model (ACF, 2012). The federal government's approach to implementing CQI was informed by a framework developed by Casey Family Programs (CFP) and the National Child Welfare Resource Center for Organizational Improvement (NCWRC), within the federal Children's Bureau. As laid out in the framework, CQI encompasses "the complete process of identifying, describing, and analyzing strengths and problems and then testing, implementing, learning from, and revising solutions. It relies on an organizational culture that is proactive and supports continuous learning. CQI is firmly grounded in the overall mission, vision, and values of the agency" (NCWRC/CFP, 2005).

The developers go on to explain that CQI is not a time-limited project or isolated initiative, but instead involves an ongoing and comprehensive process in which an agency makes decisions and evaluates progress. CQI extends beyond QA, shifting organizational focus from simple compliance to continuous learning about practice and outcomes (NCWRC/CFP, 2005). Some of the benefits include evaluating family engagement, detecting quality of services, assisting in the identification of policy and procedures that need updating, identifying targeted training opportunities, and assisting in the supervision of social workers. The meaningful and active engagement of key stakeholders (e.g., staff, children, youth, and families) as partners is critical to the successful implementation of CQI (NCWRC/CFP, 2005).

CQI systems help align the agency's practices, procedures, policies, training, and services with mission, vision, and values. For example, through CQI processes, an agency whose mission reflects a strong focus on family engagement may receive consistent feedback from consumers that families do not feel valued and included. To ensure that the agency is adhering to its mission, service practices would need to be changed to be more family-centered with a strong focus on promoting family engagement. Developing and implementing a practice model, or a conceptual map of how an agency will operate and partner with consumers and stakeholders, provides an opportunity for states and local agencies to align their mission, vision, values, policies, and practice

THE CALIFORNIA CONTEXT

Since the cases in this casebook emerged from research in California, an under-standing of the specific policy, demographic, and programmatic context in the state is important. All states that receive federal child welfare services funds (title IV-B of the Social Security Act) or foster care funds (title IV-E of the Social Security Act) must adhere to the same federal requirements. However, each state has a degree of latitude in the implementation of those requirements through state legislation and policy. California operates its child welfare system as a state-supervised, county-ad-ministered system, in which services across the entire child welfare continuum, ranging from investigations of child abuse referrals to post-permanency activities, are delivered by local county governments (Reed & Karpilow, 2009). California also has a relatively intensive court oversight role at the individual case level with each party (parents, child, county) generally having its own legal representation.

In 2001, California passed the Child Welfare System Improvement and Account-ability Act (AB 636) that was modeled after the federal CFSR and requires counties to develop their own improvement plans. The California statewide system requires the completion of a County Self-Assessment (CSA) that includes 1) a Peer Review (PR), 2) development of a five-year System Improvement Plan (SIP), 3) the submission of annual SIP Progress Reports, and 4) quarterly monitoring of the SIP strategies and their impacts on the county's child welfare outcomes (CDSS, 2018). With technical assistance provided by the California Department of Social Services, each county in California develops a county-specific plan of action, one that is aligned with the county's mission and values and reflects the specific needs of its community. Con-sistent with the principles of CQI, the quarterly review processes and annual SIP Progress Reports require analysis and reflection in order to promote continuous learning in the counties (CDSS, 2014).

CQI and Case Review in California

In order to move toward integrating case reviews into a CQI model, California implemented and funded holistic, system-wide child welfare service (CWS) case reviews in 2015. All counties now have staff trained to 1) conduct ongoing case reviews, 2) perform first-level QA, 3) identify areas where improvement is needed at the county level with respect to federal requirements and systemic issues, and 4) use the findings to inform overall state performance. The CQI process of reviewing cases at the qualitative practice level (i.e., What occurred in the home visit and what were the results?) as opposed to the quantitative level (i.e., How many home visits were conducted) offers child welfare staff and social work students a model for developing practice-based evidence to strengthen their practice (CDSS, 2015, 2016).

California Demographics

Within the United States, California has the largest population, including close to 9.5 million children and nearly 60,000 children and young adults (up to age 21) in out-of-home care. It is highly diverse with respect to language, race, and ethnicity, and is home to the largest minority population in the country, including over 100 federally recognized Native American tribes. California comprises 58 counties, each governed by an elected Board of Supervisors. Local jurisdictions vary from large urban areas like Los Angeles and the San Francisco Bay Area to very rural northern and central areas of the state (CDSS, 2015, 2016).

Programmatic Context

In California, counties administer child protection programs and services in response to locally determined community priorities and needs, while ensuring compliance with state and federal regulations. Since the mid-1990s, California has prioritized placing children removed from their parents with relatives or "non-related extended family members" (NREFMs) who are adults with a family-like or mentoring relationship with the child. Typically, about 40 percent of children in foster care at any given time in California are placed with relatives or NREFMs (Webster et al., 2017). Consistent with the priority given to family connections, California's statutory framework provides an exception to the federal requirement to terminate parental rights after 24 months in care, and California courts are generally reticent to terminate parental rights unless a prospective adoptive family is identified. As a result of this policy, distinct from many other states, there are not many children in California awaiting adoption for whom parental rights have been terminated.

County child welfare agencies provide an array of supportive services, to the extent possible, to children and young adults in out-of-home placements (related and non-related caregivers as well as congregate care settings). In addition, agencies offer preventive and supportive services to families who are at risk of having their children removed from their homes. While county child welfare agencies in California are the primary governmental entities charged with addressing child abuse and neglect, they also contract with a wide array of nonprofit and private service providers in order to meet local needs (CDSS, 2015, 2016; Reed & Karpilow, 2009).

As previously noted, child welfare agencies work with numerous mandates that play a role in practice and decision-making and are part of the broader context for understanding child welfare cases. Federal and state mandates, data measures and targets, as well as accompanying funding (and limitations and sanctions) can be significant factors in individual case decision-making, services, and outcomes, if sometimes only indirectly. For example, federal law contains requirements about 1) required elements in a family's case plan, 2) limits on the amount of time parents can be provided services aimed at reunifying them with their children, and 3) timing of actions to terminate parental rights if parents are unsuccessful in their efforts. California, as is common in other states, adds additional mandates which may also impact case decision-making and outcomes. For instance, California law enumerates circumstances in which efforts to reunify need not be provided, or when the federal time limits on reunification efforts can be exceeded or shortened. There are undoubtedly times when the goals developed for a case (based on assessment, family circumstances, unique child needs, or the preferences of the court) may be at odds with such mandates.

Risk Assessment and Practice Models

Managing safety and risk in child welfare is a complex undertaking. Social workers are informed by experience, expertise, and compassion when making judgments related to child risk of abuse or neglect (Carnochan, Rizik-Baer, & Austin, 2013). However, the assessment of risk by child welfare workers may be inaccurate, and workers may reach different conclusions based upon the same facts (Dorsey, Mustillo, Farmer, & Elbogen, 2008; Rossi, Schuerman, & Budde, 1996, 1999). Studies have found that the failure to provide social workers with structured tools to support assessment and case plan development can result in uneven service delivery and inappropriate decisions for children and their families (Baird & Wagner, 2000). Risk assessment systems enable child welfare agencies to formalize and structure the decision-making process in which child welfare workers engage when they assess child safety, the protective capacity of parents, and the risk of future maltreatment (Baird & Wagner, 2000).

Standardized assessment tools, used for almost two decades in California, aim to ensure that families are systematically assessed for safety, risks, and needs throughout the life of the case. In addition, the use of the tools promotes a uniform and consistent practice of assessment for each social worker, as well as providing for consistency in service delivery and child protection throughout the state. California uses the Structured Decision Making (SDM) suite of assessment tools developed by the Children's Research Center (CRC), a division of the National Council on Crime and Delinquency (NCCD). The tools are designed to support and enhance the existing clinical knowledge and critical thinking of county staff and are not meant to replace the experience, training, and education of social workers, supervisors, and agency management. In addition, the tools provide specific written documentation of the review, evaluation, and decisions made in the case that are useful in the event that future issues arise (ACF, 2016; NCCD/CRC, 2015).

The primary SDM tools in use in California include

- The Hotline tools which are intended to promote consistent and objective screening decisions statewide. These tools help workers evaluate whether a referral should be investigated in person and the level of priority of the response (immediate versus 10 days).
- The Safety Assessment which evaluates the child's immediate safety in the home and should be completed within 48 hours of the initial in-person investigation.
- The Risk Assessment which assesses the risk to the child's safety in the future. The tool is meant to be completed after the investigation is complete (within 30 days of the initial in-person investigation) and should inform the decision to close a referral or open a case for services (ACF, 2016).

Additional tools include a Family Strengths and Needs Assessment, Substitute Care Provider Tool, and Reunification Reassessment (ACF, 2016).

The California Child Welfare Core Practice Model

To further strengthen child welfare services, California has developed and is implementing a Child Welfare Core Practice Model (CPM) (CalSWEC, 2016). The CPM integrates and draws upon existing practices used in California and other jurisdictions, including the practice model developed pursuant to the *Katie A. vs Bonta Settlement Agreement*, the federal Permanency Innovations Initiative (Children's Bureau, 2014), Safety Organized Practice (Meitner & Albers, 2012; NCWRC/NRC, 2008), and many other existing practices implemented by California counties in the preceding decade. This framework has guided the development of values, casework components, practice elements, foundational practice behaviors, and leadership behaviors by incorporating evidence-informed and best practices from across the field. It is built on a theoretical framework that incorporates current orienting and bio-developmental theories, intervention theories, and organizational theories (see Figure 1.1).

The California Child Welfare CPM has six casework components that describe the key activities involved in child welfare services (CalSWEC, 2016):

- Prevention—focusing on reducing risk factors and strengthening or increasing protective factors in families.

FIGURE 1.1. California Child Welfare Core Practice Model (CalSWEC, 2016)

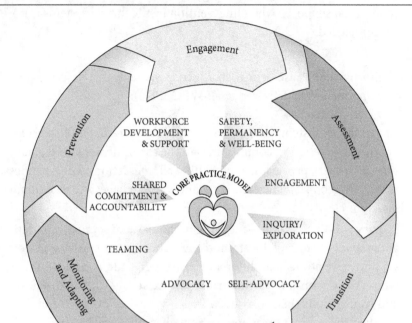

California Social Work Education Center, https://calswec.berkeley.edu/sites/default/files/casework_components_p4.pdf. Copyright © 2016 by Regents of the University of California.

- Engagement—partnering with families in making decisions, setting goals, and achieving desired outcomes; based on the principle of respect—communicating openly and honestly with families in a way that supports disclosure of preferences, family dynamics and culture, and individual experiences.

- Assessment—a continuous process of discovery with families that leads to better understanding of the events and behaviors that brought the children and families into services.

- Planning and Service Delivery—working with the family and their team to create and tailor plans to build on the strengths and protective capacities of the youth and family members.

- Monitoring and Adapting—the practice of continually monitoring and evaluating the effectiveness of the plan while assessing current circumstances and resources.

- Transition—the process of moving from formal supports and services to informal supports, when intervention by the formal systems is no longer needed.

The California model also defines six practice elements that describe "how" the casework components are delivered (CalSWEC, 2016):

- Engagement—listening to and respecting the voice of families, tribes, youth, caregivers, and communities in the assessment, planning, and service delivery processes; approaching all interactions with openness, respect, and honesty; using understandable language; and describing our concerns clearly.
- Inquiry and Exploration—engaging in inquiry and mutual exploration with the family to find, locate, and learn about other family members and supportive relationships children, youth, young adults, and families have within their communities and tribes and exploring with children, youth, and young adults their worries, wishes, where they feel safe, and considering their input about permanency and where they want to live.
- Advocacy—advocating for services, interventions, and supports that meet the needs of families, children, youth, and young adults and promoting the use of effective, available, evidence-informed, and culturally relevant services, interventions, and supports.
- Teaming—working in partnership with families, communities, tribes, and other professionals and service providers and relying on their strength and support to help the family meet their underlying needs and build an ongoing circle of support. This involves demonstrating respect, following through, and talking about and agreeing on team roles and team dynamics.
- Accountability—working to achieve positive outcomes for children, youth, young adults, and families in the areas of safety, permanency, and well-being involves measuring our practice against identified system goals and seeking continuous improvement.
- Workforce Development and Support—supporting the workforce by offering professional development opportunities, leadership, supervision, coaching, and workload supports that facilitate a healthy and positive workforce and foster a learning community.

Each element is further defined and operationalized in practice and leadership behaviors that guide practitioners, managers, and leaders in serving families, youth, and their supportive communities and tribes (CalSWEC, 2016):

- Practice behaviors include being willing to engage in open, honest, clear, and respectful communication, and to be held accountable for one's practice and leadership. Practice behaviors reflect fundamental elements taught in social work practice courses, including engagement, assessment, teaming, service planning/delivery, and case transitions.

  Example: Demonstrate an interest in connecting with the child, youth, young adult, and family and help them identify and meet their goals.

- Leadership behaviors reflect elements of macro social work practice, including engaging colleagues and stakeholders in a supportive manner; inquiring and exploring how best to lead; teaming with colleagues, community partners, and other stakeholders to implement the Model; advocating for inclusive processes and culturally responsive services to clients; and eliciting feedback about how to hold all parties accountable for the implementation, evaluation, and policy changes needed to sustain the CPM in an agency.

  Example: Establish and maintain regular and frequent communication to encourage an active partnership that engages staff at all levels in implementation and system improvement activities.

To ensure continuity in learning, the Model's basic concepts have been woven into the fabric of the California Child Welfare Core Curriculum 3.0 for the state's in-service training programs, especially to educate newly hired social workers about this new foundational approach to child welfare work throughout California. Beyond training social workers in the practice model, a multi-faceted implementation strategy is being employed to strengthen and support county leaders in order to help them make local organizational and system changes necessary to support the implementation and sustainability of the practice model (Hernandez, 2017).

DOCUMENTATION IN ACTION:
THE COURT REPORT AND CHILD AND FAMILY SERVICES REVIEWS

In addition to establishing a national framework for child welfare performance, ASFA also stressed the essential role of the court in meeting the mandated goals of insuring that children were safe, were returned to their parents in a safe environment as soon as possible, and that their needs were met while in the care of the state. Courts were mandated to examine local judicial processes both in terms of strengthening oversight and supporting specialized training for the lawyers representing children and parents. Separate funding was appropriated to each state for training for judges, lawyers, and social workers. As a consequence, the level of legal practice and judicial expertise in this area of law was elevated nationwide.

As more attorneys entered this area of practice, accompanied by requirements for specialized training, and as judges became more skilled and experienced in this area of law, juvenile dependency proceedings shifted from a relatively informal setting to a more traditional courtroom model. Attorneys utilize their skills and training as advocates. National organizations of lawyers for children and parents arose and became sources of online training and resources for even solo practitioners in small communities. Although it is common for the standard of practice to be more relaxed than in civil or criminal courts, the ethical duties of the attorneys include the same high level of advocacy on behalf of all clients. Social workers who present the case for the county or state also become the key witnesses for or against the desires or best interests of child and parent clients, which subjects them to the same rigorous examination as witnesses in any other courtroom.

The Court Report

The social worker's report to the court is a form of advocacy on behalf of the child's right to safety, permanency, and basic well-being; it is the foundation of the child abuse and neglect case presented by the state or county in juvenile dependency court proceedings. The content of the court report includes case documentation that is assembled and composed by the social worker that dates from the initial referral of the child and family to the child welfare agency to the present. This documentation includes the results of child welfare practice assessment tools from which the social worker makes recommendations to the court regarding findings and orders to be made at each hearing. For court reports, good documentation links information, assessment, and recommendations to the required findings which the court must make. In order to present the documentation in a persuasive form to the court, it is important to know about the specific orders and findings that the court is required to make or can make at each hearing.

It is also important to document child welfare assessment and decision-making tools that were used in reaching the recommendations that are made to the court. This helps to establish the credibility of the social worker's recommendations as well as avoid potential charges of arbitrariness and bias. Documenting how the information was gathered (e.g., in meetings with the parent, conferences with service providers, family team meetings) also reinforces the credibility of the social worker's assessment of the family's readiness for reunification. By statute in California, in contrast to most civil and criminal proceedings, the court report can include hearsay evidence from multiple sources, including written reports and interviews from third parties that are not testifying before the court. Although the statute does allow counsel for any party to object to all or part of the report and requires the source of the third-party information to appear for cross-examination, the preparer of the report is typically the only witness testifying about the content of the court report.

The breadth and scope of the documentation in any one case can be extensive. The increased number of those with recognized legal interests in these proceedings (e.g., foster parents, grandparents, adoptive parents, and Court Appointed Special Advocates) has contributed to the demand for extensive documentation. In addition, the increased complexity of child welfare practice (e.g., recognizing and responding to child trauma associated with child abuse and neglect, the trauma related to removal from a parent, and inter-generational trauma experienced by the parents) requires more careful and comprehensive documentation.

For the child welfare worker, the demands for time to invest in documentation within the hierarchy of job responsibilities has shifted from a historically low position to a significantly higher position, where it can consume more time than working directly with children and families. Understanding what is necessary for documentation requires understanding the ultimate purpose of the documentation. The court report is a professional document that represents the child welfare agency and the county or state, but it can receive insufficient attention in the midst of the demands of high caseloads, crisis management, and staff turnover.

Documentation has multiple audiences and purposes beyond making recommendations to the court, such as persuading parents to participate more actively in their case plan, attend substance abuse treatment, and engage in parent/child counseling. Attorneys can become partners with social workers in helping parents understand the significance of a case plan and how legal requirements can result in termination of their parental rights if their progress on their case plans is not adequate or timely. Documentation can also demonstrate the agency's support of foster parents by advocating for compensation for transportation costs, family counseling, or regular respite care. Given these additional functions, it is important to ensure that court reports make the connection between remedying the reasons for removal and assessing readiness for family reunification or an alternative permanent plan.

Documentation in Child and Family Services Reviews

As a result of ASFA, case file documentation took on new importance, and state statutes began to define the level of sufficiency of documentation for specific purposes, such as case plans. In addition to documentation for court reports, the CFSRs depend heavily on documentation created by child welfare workers. Reviewing individual cases involves understanding the history of the case through documentation and interviews with key case participants, including social workers, youth, parents, and caregivers. The documentation in the case file, including case contact notes, assessments, visitation observation summaries, and court reports are all examined for the purpose of answering specific questions from the Onsite Review Instrument (OSRI) and assessing agency practice according to the national outcome measures of safety, permanency, and well-being. Interviews are conducted with key case participants to create a complete picture of each case. Conflicting information found in documentation and interviews can lead to the assessment of noncompliance or needs improvement in an area of practice. The findings from the case reviews are required to be used to establish county goals for improving the county child welfare and juvenile probation systems and are integrated with the statewide CQI strategies.

In summary, the documentation collected and compiled by the agency child welfare worker as well as the professional assessment of that documentation can provide the foundation for the public's commitment to improving the child welfare system. In this casebook, we have drawn on multiple types of documentation to create the cases. The goal is to provide an opportunity for learning that is grounded in the reality of child welfare practice and consistent with the mission and vision of child welfare services. Learning from real-life cases can demonstrate the "explicit link connecting the agency's policy, practice, training, supervision, and quality assurance with its mission, vision, agency values, and strategic plan" (NCWRC/ NRC, 2008, p. 1). In the next chapter, we build on this discussion of documentation and explore its value for learning about child welfare practice.

② Overview of the Cases

In this chapter, we first discuss the value of case-based learning as a means to link theory to everyday practice. We then provide an overview of the basic content of the cases, describing how we chose the cases and how they were created using child welfare case record documents. We then discuss the purposes of case record documentation and some guidelines for documentation practice. The chapter concludes with reflections on the prevalence of traumatic events within the cases, and offers suggestions for ways to respond to experiences of secondary trauma and address the potential for bias. Appendix A provides materials designed to help instructors incorporate the cases in an array of case-based learning approaches, while Appendix B contains a matrix that summarizes key case characteristics and related interventions for the cases and can be used to facilitate case selection for teaching purposes.

CASE-BASED LEARNING

One of the unique aspects of case-based learning is the opportunity to link real-life situations with the theories and practice principles identified in the literature. Case-based learning provides a venue for exploring the multiple aspects of practice wisdom, complementing what may emerge in the supervisory and mentoring processes that take place during field instruction. In essence, practice wisdom is a complex blending of knowledge, skills, and experience that seeks to combine action and reflection. As Birren and Fisher (1990) note, wisdom is tested by circumstances in which we need to decide what is changeable and what is not. Wisdom brings together previously separated processes of logical knowing with uncertainty and reflection. It also relies on interpersonal exchanges in order to develop the ability to balance facts with questions about ambiguous situations while probing for truth and avoiding rigidity. Sometimes asking the "right question" can be more important than searching for the "right answer" (Birren & Fisher, 1990). Klein and Bloom (1995) note that practice wisdom includes a set of principles that incorporate the values of the worker and the profession, and serves as rules to translate empirical knowledge, prior experiences, and other forms of knowing into present professional actions. Cases also provide a unique opportunity for learners to reflect critically upon the use of practitioner standards and guidelines for decision-making behaviors (adapted from Austin & Packard, 2009, pp. 217–219).

THE CASES: CONTENT AND CREATION

The cases were identified and developed as part of a five-year, multi-county study that sought to explore and describe child welfare practices using the case record data created by child welfare workers in their daily practice (Henry, Carnochan, & Austin, 2014). The study team extracted over 5000 documents related to a total of 180 cases. In addition to the summary reports provided to the participating counties, publications of specific analyses conducted as part of the study have described multiple aspects of child welfare services, including skillful practice with older youth (Carnochan, Weissinger, Henry, Liner-Jigamian, & Austin, 2018), court report practices related to parental substance use (Henry, Liner-Jigamian, Carnochan, Taylor, & Austin, 2018), and practice supporting children who have experienced complex trauma (Taylor, Battis, Carnochan, Henry, Balk, & Austin, 2018). Based upon this research, 20 cases were developed for this casebook. The cases highlight the diversity of children, youth, and families that participate in child welfare services in the state of California. The families discussed in the cases are typical of what might appear in the caseload of child welfare social workers or might be presented in juvenile courts. The 20 case studies demonstrate how social work professionals interact with families within this context and illustrate the lessons that are learned in the field. The cases focus on the role of the social worker who represents the foundation of the legally mandated "service" that is offered to parents to help them provide a safe and stable home for their family.

In selecting cases to include in this casebook, we focused on capturing recent practice as well as a range of case types and outcomes, including voluntary and involuntary family maintenance, family reunification, adoption, legal guardianship, and long-term permanency planning. Some cases we reviewed had reached closure, while others were still ongoing. This scenario is common in child welfare practice, where child welfare workers may be assigned a case that is ongoing, requiring them to quickly gain an understanding of the family, the case plan, and service goals, based upon the case record documentation. In order to maximize the opportunities for learning from these cases, we also sought to highlight cases that represented the multiple complex and intersecting challenges that are often experienced by families involved in child welfare services. As a result, a number of the cases do not illustrate the family strengths or positive outcomes that are equally important to an understanding of the child welfare system.

The cases were developed by reviewing the key narrative documents created by child welfare workers, starting at the time when the child welfare agency received the referral that the child might be experiencing neglect or abuse. We read each document, identifying the primary individuals who played a role in the family's life; capturing the events, actions, and services involved; and creating a detailed timeline. The documents reviewed included 1) referral notes, 2) investigation narratives, 3) case contact notes, 4) court reports, and 5) case plans. Each case contains a detailed description of the composition of the family, the case narrative, and suggested questions for "case discussion." The cases note the fictitious name of the primary child at risk, summarize the initial risks and harms, and provide information about the outcomes of court hearings. Where applicable, each case description includes a description of the efforts to find a placement (or home) for the child at the center of the case. Although efforts have been made to limit the number of references to California-specific programs, initiatives, and services, some are retained as an essential element of the case. Appendix A offers strategies for instructors and students to identify parallel and contrasting features of the local child welfare context in which they study and practice, and the Glossary provides information regarding case features that may be specific to California.

CASE RECORD DOCUMENTATION

The practice of documenting in the social services, including child welfare, serves multiple purposes. While accountability and risk management have become dominant, case record documentation can also assist caseworkers in both reflective thinking and client engagement. Documentation can provide case continuity and communication among professionals; assist in assessment, service planning, and service delivery; inform agency and other decision-makers; assist with supervision; and provide information for research and service evaluation. While the content of records varies by agency and context, most documentation guidelines recommend documenting assessments, social histories, service plans and activities, progress notes and outcomes, contact information, rationale for decisions and judgments, critical incidents, referrals, and opening and closing summaries. Contemporary recording frameworks typically propose problem-oriented, structured formats and outline clear, succinct, and objective writing standards.

Given the focus on accountability, the contemporary literature focuses on the importance of documenting services as a way of meeting administrative, funding, and regulatory standards of service related to ethical issues and risk management standards (Ames, 1999; Askeland & Payne 1999; Cumming et al., 2007; DePanfilis & Salus, 2003; Garrett; 2012; Gelman, 1992; Kagle, 1983; Kagle & Kopels, 2008; Martin & Moriarty, 2012; McDevitt, 1994; Reamer, 2005). Records serve as a tool to protect both clients and practitioners in court hearings, lawsuits, or ethics complaints

(Ames, 1999; DePanfilis & Salus, 2003; Garrett, 2012; Khoo, 2004; McDevitt, 1994; Murray & Humphreys, 2014; Reamer, 2005; Stephenson-Valcourt, 2009–2010). Beyond compliance and accountability, when workers can describe what they do and provide a rationale for their actions, it creates a knowledge base for the profession and allows policy makers in child welfare to identify promising practices (Zeira, 2014). Using and modifying case records can promote evidence-informed practice and knowledge development for child welfare practices (Khoo, 2004; Martin & Moriarty, 2012; Reilly, McKelvey-Walsh, Freundlich, & Brenner, 2011).

Kagle and Kopels (2008) synthesize the empirical research related to documentation and suggest the following principles to inform and guide documentation practice:

Accountability
- Balance between competing goals of accountability, practice improvements, efficiency, and client privacy
- Risk management in terms of compliance with agency policy, legal standards, practice guidelines, and professional ethics
- Accountability focus on service delivery, impact, and outcome

Content
- Focus on the mission where case content is relevant to the agency mission or program objectives
- Objectivity related to the presentation of information that is fair and impartial, and that includes observation, sources of information, criteria used in assessment, and appraisal
- Urgent situations requiring full documentation of emergencies or crises
- Exclusion of information that is not pertinent to purpose, goals, or outcome of service
- Exclusion of irrelevant, extraneous, opinion-based, or speculative information

Client Interests
- Client involvement related to the documentation of the client's role in all aspects of the process
- Cultural context—inclusion of cultural factors influencing the client situation or service

Staff Utility
- Currency (records kept current with periodic reviews and updates)

- Access (information is written with the assumption that anyone may have access to it)
- Usability in the form of reader-friendly organization of records, usually chronologically
- Rationale provided for all service decisions

ADDRESSING THE POTENTIAL FOR BIAS AND SECONDARY TRAUMA

In this casebook, the reader will encounter families who have come into contact with child welfare services presenting a complex constellation of challenges for the social worker. These families often live in poverty conditions or experience multiple episodes of inadequate housing, unemployment, and inadequate access to health care. Many have experienced mental health problems and have abused alcohol and/or illegal substances. In addition, many of the families have had prior contact with the child welfare system or have substantial involvement with the criminal justice system. The individuals described in some cases have engaged in behaviors that you may find distressing or very problematic. It is important to pay attention to how you respond, noticing if you find yourself judging some individuals in negative ways. Contemporary social work depends on consistent and authentic engagement with parents, children, and extended family members in all aspects of the case. Engagement with families requires compassionate responses as well as direct, respectful, candid discussions.

Many child welfare cases involve similar events and experiences, including neglect, substance abuse, mental illness, homelessness, domestic violence, and exploitation. These child welfare cases may resonate with anyone that has received child welfare services, been in foster care, or who has experienced similar difficulties and challenges within their families. As with other experiences that are part of participating in an MSW program, such as sitting in an agency lobby in order to understand how it would feel to be a client, reading these cases may trigger many emotions. If you find that you would like support with respect to managing these emotions, we suggest that you talk to your instructor or contact your university health service or employee assistance program. We respect the resilience of individuals who have experienced this kind of trauma, and we appreciate the compassion of those who have not. For everyone who reads these cases, we hope that the learning value is evident.

Calvin R.

3

Calvin R. is a six-year-old boy neglected
due to parental substance use

FAMILY CONFIGURATION

Household Members	Other Family Members
Calvin: age 6	Four older siblings: do not reside in the home with Calvin
Older brother: age 9	
Mother: age 37	

INITIAL RISKS AND HARMS

Calvin (6) and his brother (9) had been attending elementary school for almost
a month prior to the events which caused child protection to remove them from
their mother. On that day, their mother had dropped them off at school right before
school started saying that she would pick them up after school and they would all
take the bus home. After school was dismissed and all the other children had left
the schoolyard, Calvin's mother had not appeared. The boys were noticed by the
school nurse who telephoned the children's emergency contact, identified as a family
friend, who responded and picked them up a few minutes later.

The next morning, the family friend brought the children to the city's transitional housing program where they had been staying with their mother for the
past month. Their mother had not returned to the shelter after taking the boys to
school and had not contacted the shelter. In the absence of any other family support
or supervision, the housing program called child protective services, which sent
an emergency response social worker. Although both boys appeared healthy, the
emergency response worker's case notes described Calvin's clothing as dirty and
having the smell of urine.

A Team Decision Making (TDM) meeting was held by the emergency response
team, but neither parent appeared. Agency records showed nine prior neglect allegations involving the family. The transitional housing program records indicated that

the mother had a history of crack cocaine addiction but lacked any other family or background information. Calvin and his brother were placed with a Foster Family Agency (FFA).

Four days after removal, Calvin's mother contacted the social worker through the transitional housing program. She explained that she had entered detox and would enroll in a residential substance abuse treatment program. The social worker told her that Calvin and his brother were living with a foster family and that she could have supervised visits by making arrangements with the foster parents. A visit was scheduled for the following week.

In a later conversation, the mother told the social worker that she felt an outpatient program would serve her better and she agreed to drug test. She stated that she had been working to stay sober but had been diagnosed with chronic depression in addition to being addicted. Although she had been sober for months at a time, when she felt overwhelmed, she would relapse as she had done recently.

FINDING A HOME FOR CALVIN

After Calvin and his brother were picked up at the transitional housing program by the emergency response social worker, they were taken to the county assessment center and placed in a foster home together.

Several family members came forward as possible placement options. All were unable to serve as a placement for various reasons. Calvin's maternal uncle was the first to contact the agency; however, he failed to follow through with the kinship care approval process. Calvin's adult-aged sister discussed placement with his social worker but could not proceed with the placement due to other obligations. Calvin had four older siblings, none of whom were adults.

Less than two months into placement, the foster mother notified the FFA social worker that Calvin's brother might have been sexually molested by another child placed in her home. She also reported that the alleged abuser was no longer placed in her home. Calvin and his brother were taken to the county's interviewing center to be interviewed about the alleged sexual abuse. A few days later, the foster mother gave a seven-day notice requesting Calvin and his brother be removed from her home. A team meeting was held at the agency to assess the boys' needs and placement alternatives. Case notes do not explain why the foster mother requested that the boys be removed from her home.

A team meeting was arranged to locate a new placement. Calvin's mother and several maternal relatives participated, including one of the mother's adult-aged cousins who applied for placement. Two days later, placement was approved with the cousin. Calvin and his brother lived with his cousin for the duration of the case review. A permanent plan of legal guardianship with the cousin was pending after the case review.

Calvin's initial service plan included regular school attendance and goals related to his education as well as a referral for counseling. Case notes reflected that Calvin and his brother were on the waiting list for individual therapy. In subsequent service plans, the counseling requirement was removed. Case notes show the social worker met with Calvin at least monthly.

COURT PROCEEDINGS
Jurisdiction/Disposition Hearing
The court found sufficient evidence of abuse to declare, by order of the court, that Calvin and his brother be made dependents of the court and ordered reunification services only for Calvin's mother.

The mother's case plan required she attend counseling weekly, complete a psychotropic medical evaluation, attend a parenting class, and participate in an inpatient program to address her substance abuse issues. A weekly visitation schedule was established for Calvin and his mother. The mother's strengths were listed in the case plan as being cooperative, receptive to services, and having provided care for Calvin and his brother for most of their lives.

After the hearing, the social worker arranged a visit between Calvin and his mother at her inpatient drug program. The following day, his mother left the program.

Although Calvin's father had not been living with the family in the shelter, he was in the same city according to the child welfare agency's family finding unit. Initially, Calvin's father said he would like to be involved and care for both boys, although he was unsure if the older brother was his son. He told the social worker he was unemployed and looking for housing. Case notes reflect multiple contacts between Calvin's father and the social worker during the first months after the boys were removed. The father said he understood a paternity test was necessary to establish his status as Calvin's father in court and said he was willing to do so. However, there is no reference in the case notes of the social worker arranging paternity testing or filing a motion to establish paternity.

Due to the father's status as an alleged rather than presumed father, the agency had not recommended reunification services. The social worker subsequently recommended that the father attend parenting classes and contact the social worker when he found housing. During the following month, Calvin's father notified the social worker that he had found housing and was also caring for Calvin's twin half-sisters. Subsequent case notes do not reflect whether the social worker arranged or attempted to arrange contact between Calvin and his father nor do they describe the nature of the relationship. Sporadic contact with the father is documented in the case notes, but there are no references to consideration of Calvin's father as a placement.

Six-Month Status Review Hearing

In preparation for the six-month status review hearing, the social worker had another face-to-face meeting with Calvin at his cousin's home. They talked about how he was doing in school and his feelings about living with his cousin. Case notes indicated Calvin said he was "okay" staying with his cousin.

The mother had made little progress on her case plan since the disposition hearing. Despite completing detox and enrolling in an inpatient substance abuse program, Calvin's mother had not started working on the other requirements of her case plan, including the psychotropic medication assessment. She was inconsistent in visiting with Calvin. The cousin who had been responsible for supervising these visits told the social worker, after a couple of months, that she was no longer comfortable doing this.

The social worker recommended reunification services be terminated for the mother. The father had not established paternity and remained an alleged father. He also had not participated in parenting classes. The social worker recommended the father's service plan be removed. The social worker recommended a permanent plan of legal guardianship for Calvin with his cousin. The mother appeared at the hearing and objected to the social worker's recommendations. The court set a contested hearing to take place the following month.

After the hearing, the social worker arranged for bimonthly supervised visits with Calvin and his mother after school at a location across from his school. Calvin's mother did not maintain contact with the social worker. She missed her first appointment after the six-month hearing with the social worker and was inconsistent in meeting with her social worker through the end of the case review. When the mother called to speak with the social worker, she refused to provide any contact information.

The following week, the social worker met with Calvin's therapist and cousin to discuss the cousin's willingness to collaborate with Calvin's therapeutic program. Agreement could not be reached and the social worker agreed to locate another therapist. Case notes reflect counseling was subsequently dropped from Calvin's service plan without explanation.

At the contested six-month status review hearing, the mother appeared and testified she was attending an outpatient program and wanted reunification services to continue. The social worker testified that the mother was not consistently attending the outpatient program, had drug tested only once since entering the program, and tested positive for two illegal substances. The recommendation to terminate services for the mother and establish a plan of legal guardianship for Calvin was maintained.

Two months later, the cousin called Calvin's social worker to say she might be interested in adoption and information was provided to her. Calvin continued to have bimonthly visits with his mother and Calvin described the visits as "fine."

Final case notes reflect that the cousin decided she was not able to adopt Calvin and preferred to be his legal guardian. The cousin reported that a problem had arisen recently involving both boys peeing into bags and hiding the bags in the house and defecating in their closets. The cousin indicated she would be meeting with the school therapist.

The cousin told the social worker that although Calvin's mother frequently called to check in on her sons, she would not talk to the boys directly. According to the cousin, the mother said she did not agree to guardianship and would "fight" the recommendation in court. The social worker's notes indicate she assured the cousin this was a stable placement for Calvin and he would not be moved from her home.

End of case record review.

DISCUSSION QUESTIONS

1. What are your initial thoughts when reviewing this case?
   - What is missing? What other information do you need to know to help the family?
   - How would having this additional information make a difference?
   - What information do you need to create a case plan or make referrals for services?
   - What resources in your community match these service needs?
2. If you had the following additional information about the father, what would you do to engage him?
   - Father (50) lives in a neighboring county but has not had contact with his children for three years. He works for a defense contracting company. Many of his co-workers have lost their jobs and he worries that he will be laid off as well. He regularly works 60-hour weeks, and when he is not at work he drinks. He believes that he is not an alcoholic because he drinks only beer, and he informs you that his wife drinks close to a bottle of wine each day. He believes that his boys are undisciplined and that they need to improve their behavior or get out of the house. He admits that he regularly spanks his 12-year-old daughter because he thinks that "she has zero manners." The father maintains that his "discipline" of his daughter is not excessive. He was so angry when his boys were taken from him by their mother that he destroyed furniture and other items in his house (Brewer, Roditti, & Marcus, 1996).

3. As the case progresses, the mother's situation changes as described below. Assess the mother's current situation and identify needs experienced by her and Calvin.

   - The mother moves into a home. On your first home visit with her, she appears depressed and is uncommunicative. Her mother, whom she felt was her best friend, has died recently. During your second home visit, the mother serves coffee and tries to maintain polite conversation. She tells you that she drinks a bottle of wine each day and that after her mother's death she has suffered from "nerves" and takes pills to calm down. She reports, "I can sit in my living room all day and nothing gets to me." The mother shows you several bottles of tranquilizers which she says her cousin who lives abroad sends to her. The mother is socially isolated as all her family members live outside of California (Brewer et al., 1996).

4. What is your perspective on the interaction of neglect and substance use in this case? Which symptoms of substance use do you observe in the case?

5. Are there individuals that play a significant role in the case that you would want to contact?

6. What, if any, concerns do you have relating to possible trauma experienced by Calvin? How would you assess for traumatic experiences?

Tina C.

Tina C. is a teenage girl sexually abused within her extended family

FAMILY CONFIGURATION

Household Members

Tina: age 14
Mother: age not specified in case record
Father: age not specified in case record
Younger sister: age 5
Older brother: age 16

INITIAL RISKS AND HARMS

On November 19 of the current year, Tina was brought to the county psychiatric inpatient center by police after she threatened to kill herself with a knife. She was hospitalized on an involuntary psychiatric hold. Initial examination described Tina as being anxious, unable to remember events consistently, and feeling light-headed and faint. Tina was diagnosed with adjustment and mood disorder. Tina disclosed that her father had sexually abused her for the past three years, including masturbation in front of her and penile penetration. On one occasion, Tina said that her mother had witnessed the sexual abuse, had done nothing, and had threatened to kill her and her sister if Tina ever told anyone about the abuse. Tina also stated that her father had asked her to entice a school classmate to have sex with him after school.

The police interviewed both parents while Tina was hospitalized. They both denied Tina's sexual abuse allegations, said Tina regularly lied, and consistently denied Tina's allegations for the duration of the case. Police determined Tina's story not to be credible and did not initiate any criminal proceedings against the father.

When Tina was released from the hospital, child welfare services conducted a safety assessment and removed Tina from her parents. Investigation revealed the family had three prior child protection referrals, including one for general neglect and two for sexual abuse earlier in the year. All the referrals were determined to be unfounded, inconclusive, or evaluated out. The parents provided names of family members as possible caretakers for Tina.

Within two weeks of removal from the home, Tina, her brother, and her sister participated in a forensic interview. During her interview, Tina gave detailed descriptions of multiple instances of sexual abuse and explained she never told anyone because her father told her "not to tell about the abuse at least 10 times."

Interviews with cousins revealed a history of sexual abuse within the extended family, including an alleged sexual abuse of a cousin by her stepfather, sexual abuse by a parent, and abuse of Tina's brother by their father, as well as a "culture of secrecy." According to one of Tina's maternal uncles, three years ago, extended family members had a meeting with Tina's father to confront him about sexually abusing Tina's brother; however, when the meeting began, her brother recanted and nothing was done. Tina told the emergency response social worker that during the summer she had been sent to live with an uncle and aunt in another city "so that she could not tell anyone" what was happening to her.

FINDING A HOME FOR TINA

After being released from the psychiatric hospital, Tina was taken to the county assessment center for further investigation and a family needs assessment. Tina comes from a large Pacific Islander community and family; however, no relatives came forward offering placement, and Tina was placed in a foster home. Tina transferred to a new school with the goal of helping her find a school where she was comfortable and could do well. In her prior schools, she had serious behavioral issues, was regularly absent, and had been expelled once.

During the four months following her removal from her parents in November, Tina ran away twice from placement, was involuntarily hospitalized three times, and moved in and out of three different placements.

COURT PROCEEDINGS

Jurisdiction/Disposition Hearing

After meeting with Tina's parents, her brother, her sister, and extended family members, it was agreed with the social worker that Tina's older brother and younger sister could safely remain with their mother and that family maintenance services would be provided. Tina's mother and Tina's brother and sister lived with Tina's maternal grandmother. Tina's parents had separated two years prior. Her father lived with a relative and continued to be the sole provider for the family.

At the hearing, the social worker asked for a continuance to review agency recommendations and consider whether Tina could be safe at home. Tina's parents continued to deny her allegations of sexual abuse. The county attorney recommended the agency petition the court to bypass services for Tina's father.

Six weeks later, the court found the allegations of the petition (sexual abuse and failure to protect/supervise) to be true. Over the objection of the agency, the court ordered reunification services for both parents and approved a case plan which included services for the entire family. A family advocate was assigned to work with the family and continued working with them for the next six months.

Tina's mother's case plan required her to participate in family therapy, individual therapy, and parenting class. Over the next six months, she attended three family therapy sessions with Tina, the father, her son and younger daughter, and several individual therapy sessions. Initially, she had problems obtaining insurance coverage for individual therapy. In June, the mother's therapist reported that the mother had stopped making progress and was "stuck" because she continued to deny the sexual abuse allegations and was adamant Tina was lying. She stopped participating in services shortly thereafter. The social worker continued to arrange visits and supervised telephone calls between Tina and her mother, but often these contacts seemed to trigger Tina running away from placement and engaging in self-harm.

Tina's father's case plan required him to participate in parenting class, family therapy, and a psychological evaluation and treatment. He attended three family therapy sessions. He told Tina's social worker he could not participate in any other services or complete family therapy due to his full-time work schedule. He had no other contact with Tina, per her request.

Tina was asked to participate in family therapy, a psychotropic medication evaluation and monitoring, a psychological evaluation, and individual therapy. She also began to experience substance use issues and was asked to attend substance abuse treatment and Alcoholics Anonymous groups. Tina continued to have problems in school and one year later was appointed a Court Appointed Special Advocate (CASA). Tina's educational rights were assigned to the CASA advocate.

The court report indicates that Tina had an array of problems in her first placement. She was expelled from her new school for offering to perform a sexual act on a fellow student. The social worker documented in her case notes that she had seen evidence Tina had been cutting herself again. Obtaining consistent medication for Tina was an ongoing problem. Tina's social worker recommended the foster parent return to the prior county to obtain refills of Tina's medications until necessary arrangements could be made in the county where the foster parent lived.

Tina was again hospitalized after expressing suicidal ideation at school. The foster mother gave a seven-day notice and, after being informed by her social worker of the notice, Tina refused to return to the foster home. A new foster home was identified in an adjacent county after a team meeting. Tina called her social worker to tell her she had been released from the hospital without her medications and was not feeling well without them. The social worker asked the foster mother to take her to a nearby mental health clinic for a psychiatric hold, but after an interview with the clinic counselor, she was released. Tina began cutting herself after returning to the foster home, and the foster parent called the social worker who requested an expedited court order for medication. The social worker arranged an emergency short-term supply of medications for Tina.

Tina transferred to a new school and the social worker submitted a referral for counseling support at school and for a psychological and medication evaluation at the local clinic.

The following week, Tina called her social worker and said the foster mother threatened her and she feared for her safety. After meeting with the social worker, Tina admitted the allegation was false and she made it because she had an argument with another foster child in the home and wanted to leave the placement. The social worker noted, "It is very interesting that Tina sabotages her school placements every time." The foster mother reported that the school informed her Tina was continuing to act up in school, trying to start fights with other girls, and was caught smoking marijuana.

One week later, the foster parent gave a seven-day notice, reporting that Tina had run away and was exhibiting erratic mood swings and manic phases. She was also smoking marijuana and using methamphetamines. Tina contacted her social worker and asked to go back to the foster home; the foster parent agreed but wanted a team meeting to discuss Tina's increasing needs and alternative placements. At the team meeting, Tina said she wanted to live with family but it was determined there were no extended family members able to offer her a home. It was agreed the social worker would seek another foster home. Tina was upset, left the room, and was hospitalized due to threats of harming herself. Tina's case plan remained the same.

On the same evening that she was placed in a new foster home, she ran away after calling the social worker and telling her she did not want to be in foster care anymore. The foster mother called the police and the social worker obtained a protective custody warrant for her arrest.

The foster mother informed the social worker she was no longer willing to care for Tina and believed she needed more structure. Within 24 hours, Tina was picked up by police and arrested on felony charges for threatening a police officer and resisting arrest; she was detained in juvenile hall.

At her appearance in juvenile court, Tina, upon hearing her social worker's report to the court, "cussed at the judge and threatened the bailiff." A team meeting was immediately convened, and it was determined that Tina's mental and behavioral health issues, which now included gang affiliation and the possibility of commercial sexual exploitation, should be assigned to the consolidated juvenile court calendar rather than to the juvenile dependency court. In the interim, the social worker requested Tina be released from custody for placement in a group home. The court agreed and the social worker drove Tina to the new group home. Tina left the group home one day before her court appearance and turned herself in to the police the following morning.

Case notes document that Tina called her social worker, telling her she was drinking and using methamphetamine, cocaine, and marijuana and "will not quit and the social worker cannot make her drug test." She also repeated she would run away again if placed in a group home. When her social worker informed Tina that she would have a visit on Friday with her mother and siblings, Tina agreed to stay. Tina also asked the social worker to arrange a visit with her uncle and said she wanted to live with her aunt. A visit was arranged the following week and continuing visits were authorized.

A referral was made for Tina to an organization serving commercially sexually exploited children, but since she was not fully disclosing about the circumstances, Tina was not eligible for formal services and could only enroll in a preventative lecture.

The following week, Tina ran away from the group home and the group home issued a seven-day notice. Tina appeared at her mother's home and her mother immediately telephoned the social worker. She stated she could not handle Tina and asked the social worker to call the police. Tina was brought to the assessment center and placed in a foster home closer to her home of origin. Case notes reflect that Tina appeared to be much happier placed closer to her family and home.

Four days later, Tina was brought to the assessment center, stating that her foster mother had threatened her because she thought Tina was flirting with her 21-year old son and indicating that she felt like harming herself. Tina ran away from the assessment center, was apprehended by the police and hospitalized.

In the following months, Tina was placed in multiple group homes, following the same pattern of AWOL episodes, detention on a protective custody warrant, and threats to family members including her brother and father. Tina was diagnosed with mood disorder NOS, post-traumatic stress disorder, and poly-substance abuse. She was prescribed Abilify and trazodone.

In Tina's most recent evaluation, Tina's mental health clinician reported to Tina's new social worker that Tina was vulnerable to becoming a sexually exploited minor because she was allegedly dating a gang member and had a positive drug test.

Tina's mother began calling her at the group home. When she called, she would often refuse to speak in English which made monitoring the calls impossible. The conversations upset Tina. Tina began to tell staff she "does not want to live." Staff decided Tina would not be allowed any telephone calls with the mother until further notice. After consulting with Tina's social worker, the group home agreed to allow Tina telephone visitations with her maternal uncle and cousin per Tina's request.

Ten days later, Tina ran away again and was picked up by police and hospitalized. In conversation with her social worker, Tina reported she was raped by her boyfriend. The social worker submitted a referral for a specialized higher-level placement. A pregnancy test was conducted and was negative. This was followed by multiple hospitalizations over the next two months. At a team meeting, it was agreed that Tina was not ready for a less restrictive placement but a referral should be made for a foster home. Tina's service plan was not modified.

Six-Month Status Review Hearing

The social worker's report to the court indicated that Tina's mother was in partial compliance with her case plan and her father was in minimal compliance. Both parents received six more months of reunification services. The parents' home situation had not changed and their case plans were not modified. Both parents continued to deny the allegations of sexual abuse. For a three-month period, September to November, Tina was repeatedly hospitalized after AWOL episodes from placement, seven-day notices from group homes, and refusals to take medication.

A team meeting convened in November concluded Tina needed a high level of care. The social worker agreed to seek approval for a residential treatment facility, Level 14 status. Tina was hospitalized the following day and Level 14 approval was received. The social worker called three higher-level residential treatment programs but each refused to accept Tina without an Individualized Education Plan (IEP). Tina contacted the social worker's supervisor and asked for a new social worker and threatened to "shoot him the next time she sees him."

Twelve months after removal, Tina was again hospitalized on a psychiatric hold. While hospitalized, she continued to threaten her social worker. Another team meeting was convened and it was decided the social worker should contact a group home where Tina had previously lived to determine if the group home might be willing to accept her.

Twelve-Month Status Review Hearing

The social worker recommended the court terminate reunification services for both parents based on their failure to complete their case plans. The court agreed and terminated services. In addition, the social worker requested appointment of a CASA volunteer to work with Tina specifically regarding her education. The social worker also requested the CASA volunteer be appointed as Tina's educational surrogate and that educational rights be transferred to the volunteer.

Tina did not appear in court; she was hospitalized for six weeks. The social worker reported Tina would like to return to one of her previous group homes but the placement refused to accept her due to her behavior. Another group home was located, but Tina refused threatening to run away or kill herself. Two weeks later, another group home was located and a new social worker assigned. Tina immediately attempted to run away but was retrieved by group home staff and returned to the group home. Four weeks later, after threatening another youth in the group home, Tina was detained by juvenile probation and placed in juvenile hall. Another group home was located where she remained for a month before she had to be hospitalized again due to uncontrollable psychotic behavior. The group home submitted a seven-day notice.

Eighteen-Month Status Review Hearing

The court report reflected Tina was living in a residential treatment program (Level 14). A new social worker had been appointed. Case notes indicated Tina was taking her medication consistently, attending summer school, and had a recent visit with her mother. Tina had been assessed for learning disabilities and had been scheduled for an IEP meeting. The agency recommended Tina continue as a dependent of the court with out-of-home placement.

End of case record review.

DISCUSSION QUESTIONS

1. Clarify information that therapists need for mental health assessments.
   - What questions should a social worker ask therapists about treatment recommendations and plans?
   - What are the key components of effective therapies utilized with abused, neglected, and traumatized children?
2. The case record states there is a "culture of secrecy" within the family.
   - What tools would you use to obtain more information about earlier family dynamics in this home/community?
   - What has occurred within this family that might undermine the safety of Tina and the other minors in her family as well as prevent people from reporting sexual abuse?
   - How might you work with the family showing your humility and sensitivity to their Pacific Island culture while helping them accept Tina's trauma and needs?
3. How do adults gain access to circumstances that allow them to seduce and sexually abuse children?
4. Parents do not have to admit that a child has been hurt or victimized in order to agree that they need to be safe.
   - List the assessment criteria used by local child welfare agencies to determine the level of risk for Tina if she were allowed to remain in the home.
   - What are possible safety plan tasks that Tina's mother could agree to which would keep Tina and her siblings safe?

5. Become familiar with case management strategies involving sex offenders.
    - How might you work with Tina's father?
    - What can you do to help Tina's mother become "un-stuck" in her therapy?

6. Tina's constant placement changes are significant to her course of treatment.
    - Explain the importance of Tina's runaway status to her remaining safe.
    - What might you be able to do to help her recognize her need for safety?
    - How would you work with a placement to respond to the dynamics that cause her to run away?
    - What steps are required to have a child admitted to a Level 14/high level residential care placement?

7. Identify local agencies and/or services for youth who have been sexually abused.
    - Choose a minimum of one agency/service. Collect agency information, interview a staff member, and identify two new ideas you have identified by being more informed.
    - Share your understanding of the needs and behaviors of commercially sexually exploited children.

8. When working in child welfare, self-care is extremely important.
    - Explain the need for self-care in reference to Tina's story.
    - What self-care do you already practice?
    - What new self-care techniques can you utilize to assist yourself in maintaining your own well-being while working with Tina and her family?

Alex S.

5

Alex S. is a teenage boy adopted by his mother years after her parental rights were terminated

FAMILY CONFIGURATION

Household Members	Other Family Members
Alex: age 15	Father: age 42, lives out of state
Mother: age 40	Paternal aunt: provides placement
	Maternal aunt: provides support for the mother

INITIAL RISKS AND HARMS

Four years ago, Alex was adopted by his mother following the death of his paternal great-aunt, who had been granted custody by the court in previous juvenile dependency proceedings. Alex, now 15, and his mother have had a difficult relationship which recently included calls to the police. In the most recent incident, Alex and his mother were arguing and the mother pulled out a knife and attacked Alex. The mother's boyfriend and the apartment manager were able to pull Alex's mother away without any injury to Alex. When the police arrived, Alex told them that his mother was high (on illicit substances) when she attacked him and fled when the police were called. When asked if he felt safe about staying in the apartment, he explained that returning to his mother's care would be "a death wish."

The police took Alex into protective custody and brought him to the county assessment center. When interviewed shortly thereafter, Alex was still very upset and refused to return home. He explained that his mother had been prostituting in addition to actively using drugs. He also stated that she had recently been in jail for stabbing her adult daughter during a fight.

Previous Child Welfare History

Child welfare agency records document 25 referrals relating to Alex and his siblings. As a toddler, Alex had been removed from his parents, declared a dependent of the court, and ultimately adopted by his paternal great-aunt after both parents failed to reunify and parental rights were terminated. When Alex was 11 years old, his paternal great-aunt died and the mother adopted Alex. Alex has multiple siblings (on both his maternal and paternal sides) who are currently in the child welfare system.

FINDING A HOME FOR ALEX

The day after Alex was removed to the assessment center, the emergency response social worker convened a team meeting; the mother's whereabouts were unknown. Alex's father, who lived out of state, participated by phone. He said that he was interested in having Alex live with him. In a private conversation with the worker, Alex said that he did not want to live with his father due to their strained relationship. Additionally, the agency had concerns about placing Alex with his father due to active child welfare cases involving other children. The paternal aunt also attended the meeting and requested that Alex be placed with her. (A background check of the paternal aunt revealed that that she could not be approved without exemptions.)

As a result of the team meeting, Alex was placed in a Foster Family Agency (FFA) home. The following day when the investigations social worker visited Alex in the new home, she noted that the overall sanitation of the home was poor, including dirty carpets and a urine smell in the house. The social worker also questioned the FFA caregiver's ability to adequately supervise the children in his care due to his limited mobility and the presence of a number of young adults "hanging out" at the home. The social worker notified the FFA social worker of these observations. Shortly after placement, the social worker began to have problems communicating with the caregiver (e.g., he failed to return her telephone calls and, despite being directed to do so, had not scheduled medical appointments for Alex). Initially, Alex denied any concerns about the foster home and stated that the placement was "OK."

One week later, Alex called the worker explaining that his placement was not working, he could not live there one more day, and he wanted to get "out." After further discussion, he said that his medication for attention deficit hyperactivity disorder (ADHD) had run out a few days ago. The newly assigned social worker became more concerned and contacted the FFA social worker. The FFA social worker had no information but expressed support for the placement. Later in the morning, the social worker received a phone call from a counselor who had visited Alex in the home and reported that the urine smell in the home was unbearable. Both the counselor and the social worker immediately contacted the state licensing board. Alex, who had been spending weekends with his paternal aunt, refused to return to the foster family home and reported that another child had urinated on his belongings. The social worker agreed that Alex could stay informally at the paternal aunt's home until the agency could complete the relative approval and exemptions. A formal investigation was started into the FFA home and Alex was interviewed as part of the investigation. Two weeks later, the agency approved placement with his paternal aunt.

During this time, Alex's mother contacted the social worker and asked to visit with her son. The first visit was supervised in the agency offices. Case notes describe the visit as very emotional and they appeared bonded. Alex was happy to see his mother and explained that "she was a good mother when she is not using."

A few weeks before the status review hearing, Alex's aunt told the social worker that she was increasingly frustrated with Alex skipping school, that she could not supervise him, and that she wanted him removed. She was also frustrated with his refusal to obey her house rules and frequent oppositional behavior. She served a seven-day notice. The social worker immediately arranged a meeting at Alex's school with the principal, his aunt, Alex's mother, and Alex. They all agreed to communicate more and work together to get Alex back on track. After discussions with the aunt and Alex, the social worker offered to authorize enhanced supportive services through a county program that provided targeted support for teenagers in placement and their caregivers, and the placement was subsequently salvaged.

Three months after the six-month status review hearing, the placement deteriorated. During an interview at school, Alex told the social worker that his aunt was "stressed out" and yelling a lot. He also said that he had just seen his mother using on the street. In a conversation with the aunt, she confirmed being stressed but stated that Alex is increasingly out of control and that his siblings steal and "smoke drugs" when they visit. In addition, she acknowledged that there was ongoing conflict among family members about accessing Alex's Supplemental Security Income (SSI) which increased her stress.

A few days later, the social worker received a threatening, rambling voicemail from the aunt in which she threatened to come to the social worker's office and "beat" her. The social worker described in her case notes that the voicemail was "shocking" and that the aunt "did not appear to be herself." The social worker spoke with one of the counselors working with Alex and his aunt; the social worker confirmed having seen some erratic behavior by the aunt. The aunt also said that she suspected that Alex was out on the streets trying to find a gun. Alex denied being involved in any high-risk behaviors like attempting to obtain a firearm or using drugs. In the same conversation, Alex denied that he was having any problems living with his aunt and repeated that he was looking forward to seeing his mother sober and was happy that she was getting back on track.

The social worker convened a team meeting the following week after receiving a call from the aunt stating that she wanted Alex "out of her home." The program counselors who had been working with the aunt reported having recently learned that she has been a Regional Center client and has significant health issues. They suggested that she may be having a bad reaction to her medication. It was decided that the aunt's physical and mental health appeared to be suffering and she was unable to care for Alex. Although Alex's mother did not attend the meeting, the social worker had reached her the previous day at a residential substance abuse treatment program. The mother said she supported finding a new home for her son and expressed sorrow that she was unable to care for Alex at this time. At the end of the meeting, the social worker was informed that the mother had left her substance abuse program that morning.

One year after Alex was removed, a supplemental petition for a more restrictive placement was filed with the juvenile court and a second jurisdiction/disposition hearing was held. Alex was placed in a second foster family home where he was familiar with the caregivers who had previously cared for one of his siblings. Alex appeared to be comfortable in the new home and was enrolled in a new school with the goal of helping him improve his grades and attendance. Alex's school-based counselor and his community mentor supported him during his transition to the new school.

During the last year of the case record review, Alex remained in this home and appeared to be doing well. Social worker notes reflected that Alex was not always satisfied with the placement, but those feelings largely related to house rules. He shared that he now had a network of positive male community role models including a mentor, an educational support counselor, and the school counselor.

The mother periodically contacted the social worker and had some contact with Alex. The mother said that she ultimately wanted to reunify with Alex but acknowledged that she needed to focus on her sobriety. Toward the end of the review period, Alex's older adult sister came forward to express interest in providing a home for Alex; however, the social worker was concerned about her ability to act as a true caregiver for Alex since their relationship appeared more like a friendship with peer-like interaction.

COURT PROCEEDINGS

Jurisdiction/Disposition Hearing

At the jurisdiction/disposition hearing, the agency recommended that the court order the mother to be bypassed for services due to her extensive child welfare history and failed reunification with Alex and siblings. The mother's attorney objected and asked the court to set a contested hearing. Alex's father, whose parental rights had previously been terminated, was not eligible for reunification services.

At the contested hearing, the social worker's recommendation remained the same, that services should not be provided to Alex's mother and that reunification efforts be bypassed and a hearing be set to determine the permanent plan. However, the mother appeared at the contested hearing, argued that the court should use its discretion to grant her services, that she and her son were very bonded, that she was very committed to her sobriety, and that having her in his life was in his best interests. The court agreed and ordered reunification services. The case plan was amended to reflect reunification services and a permanent plan goal of reunification. The mother testified that she was now in a sober living home and was working hard on her sobriety. She also said that she wanted Alex to live with his father but agreed to his living with his paternal aunt in the interim.

Following the hearing, a family finding and engagement social worker was assigned to locate extended family members should reunification fail, and the case was transitioned to the family reunification unit.

Case Plan Progress

Throughout Alex's dependency, his mother was consistent in her desire to reunify with him. Prior to the contested jurisdiction/disposition hearing, she called the investigations social worker and stated that she wanted to reunify with Alex and would do what was necessary. She admitted that previously she had been actively using, but she now had some time sober and was staying in a sober living environment. She also stated she wanted Alex to live with the father, but she supported placement with his paternal aunt in the interim.

The case plan objectives for the mother were that she maintain sobriety; express anger appropriately; avoid criminal activity; show her ability to live free from drug dependency; interact with Alex without physical abuse or harm; maintain a suitable residence for Alex; meet Alex's physical, medical, emotional, and educational needs; and be nurturing and supportive during their visits.

She was responsible for consenting to a psychological evaluation including a caregiver competency component, participating in weekly general counseling, completing a teenager-focused parenting education program, drug testing at least weekly, and completing an inpatient substance abuse treatment program.

The mother immediately began working on her case plan and visiting with Alex and shortly after underwent drug detox. During the six months after removal, she visited with Alex regularly, attended his medical appointments, and talked to Alex about his progress in school and met with his teachers. According to case notes, they made "positive strides to improve their relationship." Overall Alex was stable and doing well in his aunt's home, aside for some struggles with truancy at school. He also visited with extended family on the weekends.

Six-Month Status Review Hearing

The social worker recommended continuing the case plan goal of "return home." The mother had made progress on her case plan objectives, regularly communicated with the social worker, and was "nurturing and supportive" during visits with Alex. The court agreed and ordered six more months of reunification services and agreed to more visits with her son as she had requested. Overnight visits were planned for the next month. When this was explained to Alex, he told the social worker that he had just seen his mother on the street and she appeared to be using drugs.

The social worker lost contact with the mother for two weeks. When the social worker located her, she confirmed that she had again entered another sober living environment, but she did not disclose a relapse. She left the program the following week. Although the mother's whereabouts were unknown for the remainder of the reporting period, she periodically left messages for the social worker inquiring about her son, expressing regret about not being able to maintain sobriety, and repeating her desire to reunify. Case notes reflect that Alex consistently told the social worker that he "loves his mother and worries about her."

Twelve-Month Status Review Hearing

At the twelve-month hearing, due to the lack of contact with the mother, her failure to work on her case plan, and apparent continued drug use, the social worker recommended that the mother's reunification services be terminated. The court approved a case plan goal for Alex of other planned permanent living arrangement (OPPLA) (foster care) with the current caregiver with continued contact with extended family members. The report concluded that the initial harms and risks which caused Alex to be removed from his mother had not subsided over time, with the mother's substance abuse emerging as the primary barrier to reunification. Although the mother did not appear at the hearing, she telephoned the social worker two weeks later and admitted recent relapses and inquired about Alex and requested visits be arranged.

Eighteen-Month Status Review Hearing

In the intervening six months, Alex had increasing problems at school, particularly related to attendance. Alex was described by his foster parent as generally doing well in the placement. In monthly meetings with the social worker, Alex described conflicts particularly with the foster mother, struggling in school, and feeling "singled out" by the foster parents followed by months of improvement in school and stability. Alex asked the social worker to contact an adult sister about possible placement. A team meeting was scheduled to discuss this possibility, but the record is unclear about whether the meeting occurred or whether Alex's sister was invited. Two months later, the mother contacted the social worker to tell her that she was still participating in a substance abuse treatment program and currently had six months sober. She supported Alex being placed with his adult sister if possible but also stated that she had been seeing him regularly and that he was being well cared for in the foster home.

Although the social worker did not change the case plan goals or Alex's case plan, a family engagement social worker was assigned to facilitate engagement with Alex's adult sister as well as locate extended family support for Alex as he transitions to adulthood.

End of case record review.

DISCUSSION QUESTIONS

1. If the father were not involved in child protective cases in another state, and appeared to be a suitable option for placement, what information would the social worker need before considering placement?
   - What process would the social worker need to follow to place Alex with his father?

2. At the end of the case summary, Alex's mother contacted the social worker and reported she had been visiting with Alex and had been sober for six months.
   - If the social worker had been aware of her progress on her sobriety, how might that information have changed the case plan and/or the outcome of the case?

3. The case summary reports that Alex is visiting extended family on weekends. How might these family members be a part of Alex's plan for independent living?

4. What other case plan activities could be added to the case plan to allow Alex to work on independent living skills?

5. If reunification services had been bypassed for the mother in the beginning, how might services and placement for Alex differ?

6. If the social worker needs to find out more information about Alex's extended family, what questions might the social worker ask of Alex?
   - Of his mother?
   - Where might the social worker go to find out more information about his extended family?

7. Consider the fact that Alex was adopted by his mother after her parental rights had previously been terminated.
   - What role might this dynamic have played in the relationship between Alex and his mother?
   - How might you work with Alex and his mother to explore this issue?

Donna S.

6

Donna S. is a two-year-old girl neglected by her
mother who is overwhelmed by parenting

FAMILY CONFIGURATION

Household Members

Donna: age 2
Mother: age 25
Older twin brothers: age 4
Younger sister: born during the case

Other Family Members

Oldest son: removed and adopted in a previous
dependency case

INITIAL RISKS AND HARMS

Donna lived in a family consisting of her mother and her older twin brothers. During
the case, the mother gave birth to another child, a baby girl.

This case originated from a referral for general neglect involving the mother's
alcohol use and her alleged failure to adequately supervise her three children which
was followed by an agreement to participate in informal family maintenance (IFM).
After several weeks, IFM was deemed unsuccessful, resulting in the removal of
Donna from her mother. Her father was not located until one year after removal,
and he did not participate in the case plan (he was serving time in an adjacent
county jail).

After the mother first met with the emergency response social worker and discussed the potential consequences for her and her children if she failed to provide
better care, she attended a Team Decision-Making (TDM) meeting and was generally
open to services, agreed to a safety plan, and was assigned to IFM. Her case plan
included individual therapy, substance abuse testing, parenting classes, and participation in a 12-step program. The general neglect allegations were deemed inconclusive.

During a home visit three weeks later, the social worker noted bruises on Donna's
body as well as bleeding sores on her face. At the request of the social worker, the
mother took Donna to the hospital. Medical staff told the mother that the infection

which had caused the sores on her face was common but that the mother hadn't addressed it promptly which made the condition more difficult to treat. The examining nurse was concerned about the bruises and ordered a skeletal x-ray, giving the mother a date to return. The mother missed two scheduled appointments. Donna spent the night at a babysitter's house and the next day had more bruises and a black eye. Donna was then admitted to the hospital and removed from her mother's care by her social worker. The primary concern at the child welfare agency shifted from general neglect to physical abuse.

Prior History and Initial Case Events

Agency records show that 20 referrals had been received in prior years regarding Donna's mother for various allegations including general neglect, physical abuse, and sexual abuse. All but two of the allegations were determined to be unfounded or inconclusive. Referrals relating to the mother's oldest son had been substantiated in a previous dependency case, resulting in his removal and adoption prior to the start of the current case.

On November 16, Donna and her brothers were riding on a municipal train with a male friend of the mother when one of the boys became separated from the others. Train police found him, interviewed the friend, and called their mother. A record check of the male friend indicated that he had failed to register as a sex offender and he was arrested. When their mother was reached, she said that she had been too tired to take the children to preschool that day so she asked her friend to take them.

The emergency response worker met with the mother and the children the same day to assess the family. The mother and the worker created a safety plan. The mother agreed to participate in a TDM meeting and to take the children for medical exams. At the subsequent TDM meeting, the mother agreed to comply with the safety plan (not drinking while caring for the children), to follow through with medical exams, and to bring Donna and her brothers to the interview center to be assessed for sexual abuse.

During the investigation, multiple referrals were received regarding the mother's supervision of the children and her substance abuse, as well as sexualized behavior on the part of the twins. All these referrals were combined into a single investigation by the emergency response worker.

When the investigation was completed, the allegations of general neglect were deemed inconclusive. The mother agreed to a referral to IFM and specific conditions: the mother was required to obtain and maintain a stable and suitable residence for self and children; stay free from illegal drugs and drug test; consistently, appropriately, and adequately parent her children; comply with medical or psychological treatment; and show acceptance of responsibility for her actions. Her responsibilities included counseling, parenting education, substance abuse testing and counseling, and attending a 12-step program.

Six weeks later, the family maintenance worker met with the mother and Donna. Donna appeared well cared for. The mother wanted to know how the case could be closed soon and they discussed continuing supervision of the children, attendance at therapy, and ensuring school attendance as indicators of her ability to parent safely.

The following month, when visiting Donna at preschool, the social worker observed bleeding sores on her lips and bruises on her forehead, back, and shins. She determined that these conditions were not consistent with child abuse and instructed the mother to take Donna immediately to her doctor. The following day, the social worker confirmed with the medical social worker at the hospital that Donna was examined and that the sores were cold sores which had not been treated. Regarding the bruises, the doctor had ordered an x-ray to rule out abuse and determine the causes of the bruising.

The mother did not take Donna to have the x-ray as directed, explaining that she had lost the referral, had no transportation, and rescheduled for the following day. The social worker reminded her that bus tickets were available. The mother also explained that she was concerned that Donna was getting bruises at preschool.

Two weeks later, the babysitter reported to the social worker that Donna spent the night with her and fell at her home. She also stated that she had concerns about the mother not supervising Donna properly, including leaving her in the care of anyone willing to take her, such as other women at the shelter. She reported that when she babysat she had seen Donna sneaking food away and eating quickly, and that Donna's mother was not feeding her.

The social worker took custody of Donna and brought her to the hospital to be examined. She informed the mother that she was removing Donna on the ground of general neglect and possible physical abuse. Donna received a cast for a broken arm at the hospital.

The next day, when talking with the social worker, Donna's mother expressed frustration and regret that she did not know how to better care for her children.

FINDING A HOME FOR DONNA

Donna's father was not living in the home at the time of the first referral nor was he part of the family maintenance plan. The mother said that she had no information about the father's whereabouts and he was not located until a year later, based on information from the mother. Child welfare staff located him in an adjacent county where he was incarcerated. The father had not been previously located due to an error in the way his name had been spelled in prior searches. After being located, he had no contact with Donna throughout the case.

After Donna was released from the hospital, the social worker discussed emergency placement options with the mother who requested that Donna be placed in the home of a non-related extended family member. Social worker notes indicate that the home was inspected and "appeared safe and appropriate."

Two weeks later, despite positive interim visits by the new social worker to the home, the caregiver gave a seven-day notice stating that she was unaware of the many responsibilities involved in agreeing to have Donna in her home. She stated that she was unwilling to transport Donna to visit with her mother or brothers, participate in family decision-making meetings, or be responsible for Donna's medical care. As soon as this was determined, Donna was returned to the assessment center. She was placed immediately in a foster home; three days later, the new foster parents gave a seven-day notice due to an unrelated allegation of abuse that had occurred in their home related to another foster youth who resided there with her own child. Donna was subsequently brought to the assessment center.

Donna was placed in a third foster home shortly thereafter, and that foster family agreed to the concurrent plan of reunification services and adoption.

COURT PROCEEDINGS

Jurisdiction/Disposition Hearing

The juvenile court found the allegations of failure to protect and abandonment to be true with respect to both parents. The finding was based on the mother's failure to protect Donna from the actions of her babysitter which resulted in her sustaining serious physical injuries deemed non-accidental and the fact that the whereabouts of father were unknown. The court determined that sufficient evidence had been produced to require that Donna be removed from the care and custody of her mother, and reunification services were offered to her mother.

The court approved the recommended case plan. The case plan was based on the family assessment which identified problems requiring intervention and possible causes including lack of parenting skills due to immaturity, prenatal drug/alcohol exposure, and failure to protect from known abuse by others. Family strengths included the mother being cooperative and willing to accept services. The case plan was largely the same as the initial IFM case plan, but it included weekly parent/child therapy as recommended by a family therapist and working with a clinician from a specialized Wraparound program for young children to enhance early development.

The child welfare agency's family finding engagement worker was assigned to contact the maternal family to attempt to arrange a kinship placement. None were able to assist for reasons including health, criminal history, and prior child protective services (CPS) involvement.

Supervised visits were arranged for the mother with Donna and her brothers at the child welfare agency twice a week. The social worker's notes about those visits indicated that the mother was not very engaged with Donna, needed prompting to initiate activities with her, and had a hard time supervising her and the twins at the same time. This social worker had to intervene frequently during the visits to avoid unsafe situations, including Donna hitting her head and running out the door. According to the case notes, sometimes Donna would ignore her mother, and she often clung to staff members. (Visitation notes by the social worker and a substitute social worker were not in agreement regarding the mother's capacity to supervise all four children during the visits. The substitute social worker was less critical, acknowledging the challenges of caring for three active children under five years of age and a newborn.)

Case Plan Progress

When Donna was first removed from her home, the mother was pregnant with her fifth child. As a result, she was often ill and had difficulty working on her case plan. The social worker agreed with the mother to delay her therapy until after the birth of the new baby. Donna's sister was born four months after Donna was removed. At the TDM meeting for the newborn, concerns were reported about the baby's alleged father who had extensive CPS involvement and criminal history. The mother agreed to a safety plan allowing him to visit the baby only in public places. The baby remained in the home and was assigned a new social worker.

Many of the social worker's concerns revolved around the mother's basic capacity to appreciate the needs of young children and appropriately monitor their safety. Twice the social worker observed the mother not using a car seat harness to secure the baby in the car; the mother was not cooperative regarding the car seat help from the social worker and rejected the social worker's intervening in her care of her children. Donna's mother admitted that the alleged father of Donna's sister had been visiting in the home. When interviewed, the twins stated that they did not want to return home from their respite caregiver because their mother was mean, locked them up when they caused trouble, and they had been hit by the alleged father of their infant sister.

At the 90-day interim hearing, at the social worker's request, the court granted an order prohibiting contact between the alleged father of the newborn and the other children in the home. Reunification services were continued for Donna as were the family maintenance orders for the newborn and the twins. At the hearing, the social worker reported that mother was in full compliance with the requirement that she not entrust the care of the newborn or her twins to the care of anyone not approved by the agency. The mother was now living in transitional housing and the social worker had provided her with a car seat, crib, and stroller through a special grant.

The social worker recommended to Donna's mother that she work with a parent advocate; she agreed and a parent advocate was assigned. Case notes reflected that a strong relationship was established and the parent advocate accompanied Donna's mother to meetings with the social worker and team meetings.

Although Donna had generally been doing well in the new foster home and the foster parents indicated openness to considering adoption, after several months, Donna's foster parents reported that they were unwilling to provide long-term care for her beyond the next status review hearing due to being overwhelmed by her need for attention and supervision and her tantrum behaviors. They reported that Donna's behaviors worsened after visits with her mother. The social worker's notes described the foster parents as appearing very stressed, clearly needing a break and needing support. After conversations with the foster parents and meeting with mental health clinicians, the social worker arranged for more mental health services, including increasing Donna's therapy to twice per week and replacing the prior therapist who was inconsistent in her availability.

Six-Month Status Review Hearing

Donna's mother's participation in her case plan during this period was inconsistent. She attended Alcoholics Anonymous (AA) groups, complied with substance abuse testing, and engaged in therapeutic visitation with Donna each week. However, the social worker had concerns about her time management, organization, and follow-through. The mother had missed several of the twins' doctor appointments as well as her own, often lost her bus passes, and double-booked visits with the social worker during therapy appointments. The social worker arranged a joint session with the mother and the family therapist to discuss her problems with time management. The mother said that she was worried about keeping track of all the people involved in the case. The family therapist agreed that she would work with Donna's mother to create a calendar and list of the key players who were supports for her.

In meetings with the social worker, the mother expressed her confidence in her sobriety and feeling more comfortable with Donna and understanding her better, but she admitted that she had struggled to complete elements of the case plan such as therapy after the birth of Donna's sister. She wanted to know whether the social worker would be recommending that Donna be returned to her at the next court hearing.

The social worker explained her continuing concerns about the mother's need to demonstrate the capacity to care for all the children and use good judgment. The case plan was amended to include a psychiatric/psychological evaluation with the requirement that Donna's mother follow up with all recommendations made by the evaluator and continue with weekly general therapy sessions with a therapist referred by the social worker. Subjects to be covered in sessions included domestic violence, substance abuse, and parenting. The mother was also required to continue to participate in parent/child therapy with all three children as recommended by the family therapist.

Although Donna's mother was described in the case notes as "inconsistent" in her interaction with Donna and supervision of the other children during their initial visits, she made sufficient progress to move from supervised visitation to unsupervised visitation at the agency. After two months of positive visiting, the social worker and mother began to discuss arranging visits for Donna at the mother's residence. The mother informed social worker that she was transitioning from a shelter to a hotel.

At the same time, the foster parents contacted the social worker notifying her that they were unable to continue caring for Donna and that the social worker should seek a new placement. One week later, the foster parents decided to reconsider and subsequently agreed to maintain the placement. On the social worker's next visit to the foster home, strong attachment between Donna and the foster mother was noted and the parents expressed their commitment.

Twelve-Month Status Review Hearing

In preparation for the hearing, the social worker set up a case planning meeting. Donna's mother requested that the parent advocate attend. Twelve months after Donna was removed from her home, the mother's ability to supervise the children during visits remained an unresolved concern for her social worker. A new concern had arisen during a recent home visit when the social worker saw alcohol in the mother's room. The mother explained that the alcohol belonged to a friend. She had no documentation of attendance at Narcotics Anonymous (NA) or AA groups and the social worker assessed her stage of recovery as "tenuous."

At the case planning meeting, the social worker described multiple concerns about the mother's progress including unstable housing, disrupted services, missed alcohol testing, alcohol found in her room, and not participating in a 12-step program. The social worker informed the mother that she intended to recommend termination of reunification services for Donna and a permanent plan of adoption and continued family maintenance for the other children. The mother was very upset and not in agreement.

In the report to the court, the social worker recommended terminating family reunification services with respect to Donna but maintaining family maintenance services for the twins and infant sister, as she had explained to Donna's mother. The mother was initially very upset and not in agreement with terminating services, but over the course of several conversations with the social worker and the foster mother, she came to accept Donna's permanent placement with her foster parents. The foster parents were committed to adopting Donna and eventually forged a collaborative relationship with Donna's mother in service of Donna's well-being.

After working with the family therapist and parent advocate, Donna's mother agreed to meet the foster mother at the foster home and reluctantly agreed that adoption would be in Donna's best interests. Subsequently, the foster mother began meeting directly with Donna's mother to discuss plans and post-adoption visitation for her and Donna's siblings. She contacted the social worker requesting help with arranging a conversation with the siblings explaining adoption and what it means for their relationships in the future. She told the social worker that she believed Donna's mother was avoiding difficult conversations and visits and that Donna was having negative behaviors as a result (e.g., bed-wetting). The foster mother asked to collaborate in the conversation and requested that the social worker follow up with Donna's mother to support her in understanding the permanent plan and handling this emotionally challenging time. The social worker scheduled a mediation to discuss further the permanent plan and post-adoption visits and called the mother to remind her. The mother was unable to attend due to transportation problems and the mediation was rescheduled.

The court hearing to determine Donna's permanent plan was calendared for the following month.

End of case record review.

DISCUSSION QUESTIONS

1. What would the social worker be looking for to determine whether Donna's siblings should have also been removed from their mother's care?
   - If their development and age played a role in their remaining in the home, what might have been important?
   - What do you see as significant situations where Donna's mother showed protective capacity which allowed her to ensure the safety of Donna's siblings when she could not ensure Donna's safety?

2. Donna's mother had one family member who was able to come forward and provide Donna's initial placement.
   - What services might have been provided to this family member to maintain Donna in her home?
   - How might these services also provide additional support and assistance to Donna's mother in her efforts to reunify?

3. Picture Donna to be a six-year-old in this situation.
   - For a child of six, what additional factors should the social worker consider and would they make a significant difference, changing her decision to remove Donna and instead allowing her to remain in the home?

4. If Donna's mother had at least two willing and capable adults to reside in the home with her and her children or if family support persons would allow the family to move into their home, what safety plan might have been put into place to maintain Donna's safety?

5. If Donna's father were not incarcerated, what steps could he have taken to provide care for her in his home?

6. What services were provided to Donna and her mother that were significant in providing safety for Donna?

    • What other services would you like to see provided?

7. What behavioral changes in Donna's mother would have supported a recommendation to reunify?

Carlo M.

7

Carlo M. is a two-year-old boy who is removed from his immigrant parents due to domestic violence and substance use

FAMILY CONFIGURATION

Household Members

Carlo: age 2
Mother: age 21
Father: age 23
Younger sister: age 1

INITIAL RISKS AND HARMS

Carlo's family came to the attention of the child welfare agency after his father was arrested for domestic violence for assaulting his mother. Carlo was not present during the incident but his sister was present with the mother. This was the first encounter between child welfare services and the family. Carlo's father, who had an extensive criminal history, including earlier arrests for domestic violence as well as alcohol and drug-related offenses, was arrested. (He was found guilty and served six months in jail.)

The following day, an emergency response social worker visited Carlo, his sister, and his mother. The mother told the worker that she did not want the father to come back to the family and guessed that he might be deported due to his criminal history. After further assessment of the home, the history of domestic violence, and a team meeting, it was determined that there was insufficient risk to remove the children at this time and that the mother should be offered informal family maintenance (IFM) to help her. The mother agreed.

Two months later, Carlo, his mother, sister, and uncle moved into a shared room in a neighbor's house. Case notes show that the mother was appropriately engaged with the children and they seemed bonded. The mother told the social worker that she and the father had separated but she was not ready for a divorce. The social worker explained to the mother what family maintenance involved and her service objectives. These included that she create a domestic violence relapse prevention plan; maintain a stable residence; meet her children's physical, medical, and emotional needs; and not permit others to abuse her children. The mother said that she understood, had support from her mother and aunt, and had enrolled in community college.

The social worker explained that she would be in regular contact and would meet regularly with her. Over the next month the social worker attempted to reach the mother by phone over 10 times and made unannounced home visits, but she was unsuccessful in making contact. The following month, four months into the case, the social worker located the mother at Carlo's daycare. The mother told the social worker that she was about 20 weeks pregnant and had sent Carlo's sister to live with her maternal grandmother out of town. (She remained living with her grandmother for the duration of the case record review and was never made a dependent of the court.) The mother's pregnancy had been difficult and she told the social worker that there was a period of time when she thought she might lose the baby. The social worker reminded Carlo's mother of the objectives of her family maintenance plan. The mother said that she was attending classes daily and had been too busy to follow through with the therapy referral or re-enroll Carlo in childcare. The social worker gave her another referral and helped with the childcare re-enrollment. Carlo was doing well in daycare.

Six months later, Carlo's father was released from jail and moved back in with Carlo, his mother, and uncle. The father had obtained his green card and Carlo's mother began helping him with his immigration status. The social worker noted in the record that the mother was doing well and that she was considering closing the case.

Three weeks later, the mother gave birth to a baby boy who was born with a positive toxicology. The mother also tested positive for methamphetamines and admitted to the nurse that she had been using methamphetamines about once a week for the past year. The hospital notified the child welfare agency of the birth and the mother's positive drug test; the agency removed the baby and placed him in foster care.

The following day, the mother met with her social worker. She explained that she did not feel like she had a drug problem, but used drugs only occasionally when she felt stressed. She had limited prenatal care and had very few provisions for the new baby. She shared that her aunt was planning to bring her and the babies to a safe place so she could leave the father.

FINDING A HOME FOR CARLO

When Carlo's mother engaged in continuing drug use and failed to attend a relapse prevention program, Carlo was placed in a foster home with his infant brother. The paternal grandmother asked that they be placed with her, but there were multiple concerns that prevented placement for approximately six months, including lack of cooperation by Carlo's step-grandfather. The foster parents had become bonded to the boys and indicated that they were available for placement as needed and felt that the transition was moving too fast. Once these issues were addressed, the children transitioned to grandmother's home over the course of a month.

Carlo and his brother remained with their paternal grandmother for the remainder of the case record review. She told the court that she was willing to provide the children a permanent home through legal guardianship or adoption if the mother was unable to reunify. The mother supported the placement because she felt that this home allowed her more time to visit. Although Carlo's grandmother appeared committed to his care, she had to be instructed about closely supervising his dietary needs and allowing him to play unsupervised.

Carlo's only service objective was to receive child-oriented services. Carlo was enrolled in a daycare program that offered him the opportunity to socialize with other children. Shortly after removal, he was diagnosed with post-traumatic stress disorder (PTSD) by the parent/child therapist. Carlo received services from a therapist on a weekly basis. However, these services required his mother's presence, and she was not consistent in attending the sessions until 10 months into the reunification phase of the case. Within two weeks of coming into care, the therapist told the social worker that he had concerns about Carlo's speech and a referral for an assessment was made. (Months before, a public referral agency had interviewed Carlo's mother who denied that he had a speech problem and the referral was closed.) The social worker ordered a screening but a formal assessment was never completed according to case records. The social worker referred Carlo for an Individualized Education Plan (IEP), but delays at the school followed by the end of the school year had resulted in the assessment not being completed. At the end of the case record review, 16 months after the initial referral to child protective services, the mother's case manager was working on enrolling Carlo into Head Start where he could receive a speech assessment.

COURT PROCEEDINGS
Jurisdiction/Disposition Hearing
The agency recommended that the court order reunification services be provided to both parents. The court approved continued placement in foster care for Carlo and his brother until the grandmother could find a larger apartment. The court ordered that all visits be supervised at the discretion of the agency. The court also explained to the parents that their children were under three years of age which required the court to terminate reunification services if they could not prove that they had remedied the circumstances leading to removal and were capable of providing for the children.

Case Plan Progress

One month after the hearing, the social worker met with the parents at a supervised visit and discussed case plans. The father's case plan centered on domestic violence and substance use. He was expected to attend a 52-week domestic violence course, a 12-step program, substance abuse counseling, and weekly drug testing. The father did not sign up for these services until three months later; he showed up for several drug tests, but he did not participate in any of the other services. The father was incarcerated periodically over the following six months. The father did not keep in contact with the social worker despite many attempts by the social worker. Case notes indicate that he denied responsibility for his actions and did not believe it was necessary to change his behavior. He denied drug use and any domestic violence. He also had not enrolled in the domestic violence classes required as a probation condition. A week after the parents met with the social worker to discuss case plans, the mother called the police due to Carlo's father threatening her and pushing her around.

Although the father was not complying with any requirements of his case plan, he visited Carlo frequently and Carlo was attached to him. Prior to the permanency hearing, the court had approved terminating reunification services for the father due to his failure to comply with any of the terms of his case plan. The father neither attended the hearing nor contested the recommendation to terminate services.

The mother's reunification case plan consisted of the same objectives identified for her during her family maintenance case. Her case plan centered on taking steps to not be victimized by domestic violence, keeping her children safe, and finding appropriate housing for the family.

When Carlo's mother failed to participate in the domestic violence class, the social worker changed this requirement to individual therapy. The mother remained inconsistent in her drug testing, and she often only completed half of the required tests in a given time period. About 10 months into the case, she tested positive for alcohol. Testing was increased to twice each week. The restraining order against the father expired because the mother failed to appear in court.

After the baby's birth, the mother suffered serious health problems requiring surgery on her gallbladder and a kidney. As a result, she did not work on her case plan for the first several months following the delivery and surgery. After the surgery, she experienced no more serious health problems.

The parent/child therapist was concerned that Carlo's mother had a clear pattern of doing well, becoming overwhelmed, and stopping services. The mother would periodically go to Mexico without informing the social worker or making arrangements with her therapist or program. Team meetings were put in place as a way to help the mother understand the behavioral pattern that was undermining her progress. The meetings included the parent/child therapist, the mother's case manager, and the paternal grandmother. The primary goal was to create a plan that helped Carlo's mother manage her responsibilities and better understand how services were intended to improve her health and bring her family together. All of the mother's subsequent drug tests were negative, and she began to actively participate in the outpatient services. Carlo's mother started to make progress on her case plan after these team meetings started, and the case manager helped her with time management and completing the many required services. Therapy was moved to the day treatment center for the mother's convenience.

Six-Month Status Review Hearing

During this period, a new social worker was assigned. During the social worker's first meeting with the mother, she showed some remorse for her drug use during her pregnancy but had not signed up for domestic violence or substance abuse classes. Social worker notes reflected that Carlo's mother did not "present as committed to services."

The social worker agreed to help the mother find a job and financial support for her baby and arranged a meeting with the Linkages program for an orientation. The mother failed to appear and later that day the social worker found out the mother had traveled to Mexico and was visiting relatives. The social worker was unable to reach her for a month.

Upon the mother's return, the social worker convened a team meeting including the mother, the children, and the paternal grandmother at the parent/child therapist's office. The social worker again explained the mother's case plan to her and the consequences of not participating in services. In addition, she was informed that all visits with Carlo would continue to be supervised until she filed the restraining order against Carlo's father and started attending all of her drug testing appointments.

One month later, upon receiving a report that Carlo's mother had been consistent in coming to appointments at her substance abuse program and continued to test negative for drug and alcohol use, testing was reduced to once a week.

During a home visit, the social worker discovered that the caregiver, the paternal grandmother, had taken Carlo and his brother to Mexico for a visit and had extended the visit without notifying the social worker. Both children appeared to be doing well and the social worker reminded the paternal grandmother that continued placement of Carlo in her home depended in part on her being in communication with the agency.

One week later, the agency that provided drug testing notified the social worker that Carlo's mother had a positive test for alcohol. The social worker met with the mother and explained that twice weekly tests would be required again due to her positive test. The mother explained that she had recently gotten a job and was working long hours. The plan was to move to unsupervised visits as soon as she had two consecutive clean tests.

Twelve-Month Status Review Hearing

At the 12-month hearing, the social worker recommended that reunification services be extended and that the mother receive six more months of services. The final team meeting that took place a few weeks before the court hearing had focused on the mother and Carlo's progress. Family strengths identified included that Carlo's mother was doing well in school, had an appointment to get her driver's license, and was spending more time with both children on her own. Carlo seemed more relaxed interacting with his mother during the visits and no longer cried when she left at the end of the visit. Concerns identified at the meeting included that Carlo's speech had regressed over the previous two months and he had become more aggressive. In addition, the mother missed three drug tests during the previous month, was still not calling to cancel appointments, and had not completed the Head Start application.

The parent/child therapist notified the social worker and the mother that if the mother missed another appointment, she would have to consider closing the case. The social worker spoke with the mother and explained the importance of this specialized therapy to her and her parenting capacity. The mother attended her appointments over the following two months; mother's therapist reported that she had been coming to therapy consistently and was working to address her feelings about the case, parenting, and her self-esteem. The therapist described her as "a young mom who lacked confidence in her instincts but was utilizing therapy appropriately." Three weeks later, the therapist called the social worker to inform her that it appeared that the mother "had turned a corner" and they had a good session. After the call, upon leaving her office, the therapist saw the mother in a car with a man holding a beer can. The mother told the social worker she didn't know he would have beer and promised that she (and the children) would never ride with him again.

During the following month, reports from the outpatient substance abuse program about the mother's attendance at classes and participation continued to be positive. The social worker assessed the case and determined that the family was ready for reunification with the support of case management from the family preservation program. The social worker met with the mother and the grandmother to discuss next steps. The grandmother explained that she was concerned about the mother's new boyfriend and her coming home late and not helping put the children to bed. The mother wanted her younger sister to live with her to help out with the children, but the grandmother did not agree. The social worker told the mother and the grandmother to try to find an apartment that could accommodate the mother and the children as well. A shared apartment would be needed for a trial visit to start.

Two weeks later, the family preservation social worker met with the mother and grandmother to discuss living arrangements. The mother raised a concern that the paternal grandmother would allow the father access to the apartment and not respect the restraining order. Grandmother was concerned that she would no longer receive foster care funding if the mother and the children reunified. The mother insisted that she wanted her 17-year-old sister to live with them. It was agreed that if the mother signed a statement that she needed her sister to help her care for Carlo and his brother that she could live with them as well.

End of case record review.

DISCUSSION QUESTIONS

1. After Carlo's sister was born, what information regarding the mother's prenatal care and drug use during pregnancy would be helpful for the social worker to know?

2. Based on the information you have on the mother's needs following Carlo's sister's birth, create a resource list of formal and informal substance abuse programs and support groups in the area.
   - Identify specific information such as eligibility criteria, referral process, cost, length of time, etc.

3. The mother reports she uses drugs when she is stressed.
   - How can you help the mother recognize her triggers and identify possible personal interventions which she can incorporate into her daily life?

4. Describe a safety plan (if any) that might have been put into place to prevent removal of Carlo's sister?

5. Based on the information provided, identify information necessary for a court report to place Carlo's sister in out-of-home care and note any information that might be missing.

6. Identify the strengths and underlying needs you recognize in this family. Note how the strengths already meet the family's needs.
   - What services will be necessary for any unmet needs?
   - What barriers do you recognize which may undermine or prevent success for the family?

7. In the case record documents, social workers use the terms bonding and attachment when describing the relationship between adults and children, often interchangeably.
   - What is your understanding of these terms? How do their meanings differ?

8. The case record indicates that Carlo's parents are immigrants, and the mother and grandparents bring Carlo and his brother to visit family in Mexico a number of times.

   - How might the social worker explore whether immigration history or cultural variables are playing a role in the case?
   - The social worker frames the trips to Mexico as noncompliance by the family; can you articulate a strengths-based perspective on these visits?

Shawna L.

Shawna L. is the infant daughter of a teenage mother
who was a dependent of the juvenile court, ran away from
placement, and possibly experienced sexual exploitation

FAMILY CONFIGURATION

Household Members

Shawna: age 1

Mother: age 17, juvenile court dependent for three years at the time of Shawna's removal, residing in a Foster Family Agency home

Maternal great-aunts: former legal guardians of Shawna's mother

INITIAL RISKS AND HARMS

Shawna's mother had been a dependent of the juvenile court for two years at the time of Shawna's birth and was still a dependent when Shawna was removed from her care a year later. Shawna's mother had been removed from her legal guardian's home due to a substantiated allegation of physical abuse by her grandfather who lived in the same home. Case notes from the mother's dependency case described problems associated with substance abuse and the possibility of emerging mental health issues. Shawna's mother became pregnant with Shawna when she was 16 years old. Case notes refer to allegations of prostitution involving Shawna's father as her trafficker.

Shawna was brought into protective custody by the child welfare agency after her mother left Shawna with friends and did not return to pick her up. The friends notified the maternal great-aunt when she had not returned by the following morning. The great-aunt picked up Shawna and called the agency.

Shawna and her mother had been living in the Foster Family Agency (FFA) home of a non-related extended family member. Shawna's great-aunts requested that Shawna be placed with this foster parent since she had known Shawna since birth and had a close relationship with Shawna's mother.

FINDING A HOME FOR SHAWNA

The social worker team agreed that Shawna should be placed in the FFA home where she had been living with her mother. The social worker left messages for Shawna's mother that there would be a team meeting the following day to discuss what needed to be done to ensure that Shawna was safe in her mother's care. The mother participated in the team meeting via phone, refused to provide an address, and said that she was not ready to meet with the social worker. She agreed that Shawna would be placed with her foster mother saying that she was unstable and unable to care for Shawna at this time. She stated that she would not attend the detention hearing because she had an outstanding warrant. She provided Shawna's father's name and contact information including an address out of state. Shortly after the detention hearing, Shawna's mother was arrested for being in possession of a stolen vehicle and remained in juvenile detention for approximately two months.

Shawna's father was unable to attend the detention hearing but spoke with the social worker indicating that he was interested in caring for Shawna and wanted services. His relatives contacted the social worker and requested placement of Shawna, but because her mother was offered reunification services, the social worker decided that it was in Shawna's best interests to keep her in a local placement.

Due to Shawna's age (under three) the social worker recommended in her report that the court order a concurrent plan of adoption at the disposition hearing and began exploring permanent plan options for Shawna if her mother failed to reunify. Shawna's current foster caregiver was willing to become Shawna's legal guardian but was not willing to adopt her. A maternal cousin came forward and indicated that she was willing to adopt Shawna and would take her into her home immediately. Due to her husband's criminal history, the cousin's home could not be approved. Two weeks later, the maternal cousin informed the social worker that she and her husband had separated, that she had moved into a new apartment, and was ready to have Shawna in her care.

Shawna adjusted well in her new home and overall was described as "a healthy and happy" toddler. Shawna was observed especially carefully because she had been born very prematurely. As a consequence, an early intervention team from the county children's hospital followed her development. Shawna was assessed as meeting developmental milestones aside from some possible language delays.

Shawna's former caregiver maintained regular contact and visitation with Shawna and her maternal cousin. Shawna was able to stay connected with her former foster mother through weekly visits and, later, through daycare at the foster mother's home. After two months, the former caregiver began to express some complaints about Shawna's home situation. Although not specific in her complaints, she asserted that the cousin might be living with unsafe people, including her former husband. The social worker assessed these complaints, interviewed the cousin in her home, spent time with Shawna who seemed to be doing well, and found no basis for further investigation.

COURT PROCEEDINGS

Jurisdiction/Disposition Hearing

The juvenile court found the petition alleging general neglect, failure to supervise, and abandonment to be true and declared Shawna to be a dependent of the court. The court agreed to continue the disposition hearing until Shawna's mother could appear, as she was in juvenile custody. At the continued jurisdiction/disposition hearing, Shawna's mother was still in juvenile custody but indicated her desire to care for Shawna and was offered reunification services. The agency requested that the court approve a concurrent plan of adoption.

Shawna's mother's case plan identified multiple causes for Shawna's removal from her mother, including her mother's delinquent behavior, her history of being abused as a child, poor impulse control, chronic family stress, and drug abuse. Shawna's mother's case plan contained the goal of reunification, with the requirements that she visit weekly, stay free from illegal drugs, drug test, demonstrate ability to live free from drug dependency, show willingness and ability to have custody of Shawna, and not break the law. She was also required to maintain a stable and suitable residence, comply with medical or psychological treatment, and consistently parent her daughter.

At the hearing, Shawna's father was determined to be an "alleged father" since he was neither present for Shawna's birth nor listed on the birth certificate. The judge stated that the father would have to establish paternity in order to request reunification services. Shawna's attorney requested that the court order visitation following the mother's release from juvenile detention. The court authorized only supervised visits at the agency office due to the mother's reported threats to kidnap Shawna.

After the hearing, the father and his relatives began to contact Shawna's social worker. The father, who was living in another state, expressed his interest in reunification services. The social worker provided him with referrals for paternity testing, as well as domestic violence, substance abuse, and parenting classes.

At a team meeting two months later, the father participated by telephone and said he was now ready to take the paternity test and wanted reunification services, but he would "not sign any papers" until paternity was established. The mother telephoned at the end of the meeting, stated that she still planned to surrender, and understood that the court could terminate her reunification services and allow Shawna to be adopted if she did not complete her case plan in as soon as 12 months.

Following the mother's release from detention the following week, she again went AWOL and her whereabouts were unknown for approximately one year. Two months after her release, the mother contacted the social worker and reported that she was on the run but planned to turn herself in to her probation officer by the end of the week. She indicated that she would rather do so than kidnap her daughter and would like to see her daughter. Her aunt reported that she had heard that Shawna's mother was prostituting in a nearby city.

Six-Month Status Review Hearing

Taking into consideration Shawna's age and the failure of her mother to meet the goals of her case plan and/or communicate with her social worker, the agency recommended termination of reunification services. The social worker testified that Shawna's mother had called her office twice during the prior six months but refused to discuss her case plan, provide an address, or arrange visits. The mother's attorney set a hearing to contest the agency recommendation that services be terminated.

The contested six-month hearing was held, evidence taken, and reunification services were terminated for the mother. The father remained an "alleged father" at this time. Court records disclosed an active restraining order preventing the father from having contact with the mother and Shawna. The hearing to terminate parental rights and establish the permanent plan of adoption was set by the court.

A new social worker was assigned to Shawna's case and a social worker from a community partner program was assigned as well as an adoption social worker.

Selection and Termination Hearing

Two months prior to the selection and termination hearing, the agency received the results of the paternity test which confirmed that the alleged father was Shawna's biological father. Case notes indicated conversations between the social worker and father informing him that he could ask the court for services if he was interested in caring for Shawna. No subsequent contact with him was reflected in the case notes.

Shawna's mother had been unreachable for almost 12 months after her release from juvenile detention. Twice the agency appeared in court describing their unsuccessful efforts to locate and serve the mother with notice of the hearing to terminate parental rights (TPR). In addition to the social worker, the adoption social worker also made independent efforts to track down Shawna's mother by contacting remote relatives, friends, and past service providers. After the social worker sent a letter to the parents notifying them of the hearing date and the agency's intention to ask the court to terminate parental rights, the mother attempted to contact the adoption social worker. A week later, the mother reached the adoption social worker. She said that she opposed the plan of adoption and would attend the hearing.

Two weeks later, Shawna's mother contacted the social worker and left a message that she would be surrendering to her probation officer to clear her warrant and intended to appear at the hearing to oppose the agency recommendations.

Shawna's former caregiver (the foster parent for her mother) continued to express concern about the maternal cousin, saying that there were numerous people coming in and out of her apartment and that the cousin's mother provided most of the care for Shawna. The following week, the social worker received a message from Shawna's aunt that the maternal cousin was in jail for resisting arrest. The cousin had been stopped by the local police for driving a vehicle with a broken taillight. Shawna and two adults were in the vehicle. The adult male in the passenger seat was arrested for possession of marijuana and cocaine found in the vehicle.

At the initial TPR hearing, Shawna's mother appeared in court, testified about her bond with Shawna, and reaffirmed her desire to parent her. She testified that she had provided exclusive care for Shawna following her birth and that during the past year she had visited twice with her daughter. (Both visits were unauthorized and unsupervised.) Her attorney filed a motion to modify the previous court orders terminating services. The motion was heard and denied. The mother also requested visits with Shawna; the court denied her request but ordered the social worker to assess whether visitation would be in Shawna's best interest after the mother was released from juvenile detention. At the conclusion of the hearing, the court remanded the mother into custody.

Regarding Shawna's placement, the social worker notified the court that the maternal cousin had been arrested for possession of drugs. The judge continued the hearing to reevaluate the appropriateness of the current placement and the concurrent plan of adoption with the maternal cousin. Following the hearing, the social worker met with the cousin. She "appeared devastated" according to the case notes and denied any wrongdoing. The cousin alleged racial profiling as the basis of her arrest and reported being unaware of the drugs found in the vehicle. The social worker continued to support placement with the cousin but requested that the cousin submit a drug test. The cousin refused stating that she no longer wanted to adopt Shawna. During a lengthy conversation, which included the specialized support social worker, they expressed concern about Shawna's well-being, stressed her attachment to the cousin, and the likely negative impact on her sense of stability and bonding. The cousin subsequently agreed to a drug test, reaffirmed her commitment to adopt Shawna, and accepted a referral for individual therapy.

At the continued hearing, the social worker reaffirmed the agency's support for Shawna's placement with her cousin and the plan of adoption. The hearing was continued again to assess the appropriateness of visitation with the mother while she remained in custody. Just prior to the continued hearing, Shawna's mother was released from custody on electronic monitoring. Within 24 hours, she cut off her ankle monitor and was again AWOL.

At the continued hearing, the agency maintained its recommendation that the court terminate parental rights of both parents and acknowledged that, due to changed circumstances, the concurrent plan for Shawna had not yet been finalized. The maternal cousin's drug test showed a positive result for cocaine. She asked that her mother (Shawna's maternal great-aunt) be considered for placement and as the adoptive placement for Shawna.

In addition, the mother's attorney raised questions about proper notification of Native American tribes pursuant to the Indian Child Welfare Act (ICWA) and indicated that Shawna's mother said she had Cherokee blood.

At the final session of the termination and selection hearing, Shawna was found to be adoptable. The social worker reported that the recommended plan was to place Shawna with the maternal great-aunt and the emergency relative approval process had been initiated. The mother's attorney requested a referral to post-permanency mediation to arrange visitation between Shawna and her mother. Regarding ICWA, the social worker reported that the Bureau of Indian Affairs had verified that Shawna's mother had no tribal identification, confirming the information given by maternal relatives.

End of case record review.

DISCUSSION QUESTIONS

1. If Shawna's mother had returned to her aunt's home and Shawna was still placed in care there, what concurrent plan would be appropriate for Shawna?
   - Explain your reason for this plan.
2. If Shawna had been placed in the custody of the child welfare agency at birth, how might her case have differed with respect to her placement, visitation, and her mother's case plan?
3. How does it complicate cases when the parent is a current dependent?
4. What could Shawna's social worker have done differently to involve Shawna's father?
   - If Shawna's father had been in the same state, how might the social worker have involved Shawna's father?
5. Which members of Shawna's family could continue to be a part of Shawna's life at termination of parental rights and how?
6. Shawna and her mother did not have the same social worker.
   - What are the pros and cons of having different social workers for them?
7. Would Shawna's mother be considered a commercially sexually exploited child (CSEC) or a prostitute? Explain your answer.
8. At the end of the case record there is a question about whether ICWA should apply.
   - If ICWA were established, how would/could that change the practice in the case?
   - What steps should the social worker have taken to determine if ICWA should apply? When should this inquiry take place?

9. Shawna had some visits with her mother that were not authorized by the social worker and were unsupervised when they were court ordered to be supervised.

- How would you address this with Shawna's placement?
- How would you address it with her mother?

Sean T.

9

Sean T. is a pre-teen boy removed from home based on
his mother's refusal to continue caring for him

FAMILY CONFIGURATION

Household Members

Sean: age 11
Mother: age not specified in case record
Younger brother: age 10
Younger brother: age 9
Younger sister: age 7
Younger brother: age 3
Younger sister: born during the case

INITIAL RISKS AND HARMS

Sean came to the attention of child protection after his maternal aunt called the
police asking that he be removed from her home. She explained Sean's mother was
not willing to care for him so she'd been taking care of him for the previous four
months. She reported that his behavior had become out of control and he was
incorrigible, defiant, and doing poorly in school. When the police called Sean's
mother, she stated Sean was no longer allowed in her home because of his behavior.
She had four younger children and could not control his behavior as well as care
for his siblings. She asked that he be placed into foster care. The police removed
Sean from his aunt's home and transported him to the county assessment center
for assessment by child protection social workers.

The previous year the child welfare agency had been involved with Sean's family
because his mother called the agency, describing Sean as "out of control," defiant,
and belligerent; she described herself as overwhelmed. At school, he was failing in
all his classes and regularly receiving detentions. Sean's mother also acknowledged
not feeling bonded to Sean, and she was unable to say anything positive about him.

She told the emergency response worker that she was not willing to have Sean live with her family. After discussions, Sean's father and grandmother agreed to take Sean into their home for a month and the agency closed the case. This was the first time Sean had spent any time with his father or paternal relatives.

One month later, Sean's father returned him to his mother's home, but Sean's mother refused to let him stay and called the police. The police threatened her with child endangerment if she did not agree to take Sean back in her home. Sean's mother eventually agreed but told Sean to look for another place to stay. Sean telephoned his maternal aunt who agreed to let him stay with her and her family.

Sean's father expressed interest in having a relationship with him throughout the case, but he did not follow through with his case plan and services. Sean's father did not have a job or stable housing for the duration of the case record review, and he never visited Sean. Sean was not interested in having a relationship with his father or being placed with him. The father did arrange for emergency placement with Sean's grandparents while the agency searched for an appropriate placement.

FINDING A HOME FOR SEAN

When interviewed by the assessment worker, Sean was emphatic about wanting to remain in the same school he had been attending and the social worker was successful in placing Sean in a nearby foster home. Sean had friends at his old school and did not want to transfer to another school. While in this foster home, his foster parents noted Sean was behind academically and was having behavioral issues at school for which he was (receiving detentions). While in the first foster home, Sean called the foster mother "mom," and told the students at school she was his step-mom. Less than two months into this placement the foster family gave their seven-day notice. They stated Sean's behavior was putting the other children in the home at risk and they did not feel it was safe for them with Sean living there. However, they had not shared these concerns with the social worker or asked for any assistance before giving their seven-day notice. Before the seven-day timeline was up, the foster parents called the social worker and stated they needed Sean removed immediately. The foster parents reported that Sean had ripped the blinds down from the windows, was very upset and had been crying. The social worker agreed with the seven-day notice, picked up Sean, and transported him to the county assessment center.

Sean's was placed in a second foster home that was also located near his school. While placed there, Sean reported that he liked the foster home but he wanted a home where English was the primary language. He also told his social worker he did not like the food the foster family served because it was culturally different from what he was used to eating. This continued to be a problem for the duration of this placement.

The social worker attempted to find another placement near Sean's previous school, where the caregivers spoke English as their primary language, and were prepared to support his behavioral needs. Two months later, the social worker found another placement that met these requirements, but Sean no longer wanted to move. Sean told the social worker he felt connected with the foster family and did not want to leave. His grades had also started to improve and he had not been suspended. Sean finished the school year at his old school, but was transferred to a new school the following school year.

Two months later, these foster parents submitted their seven-day notice over the phone. The foster parents stated that they wanted to keep Sean but his behaviors at home and school were beyond their capacity to control.

After it was agreed a new placement would be located for Sean, a team meeting was held but no placements were available. It was agreed Sean could stay with his aunt for up to 20 days as an emergency placement. One month later, Sean was placed in his third foster home. Sean struggled in this placement with respect to his behavior in school and was suspended multiple times. Sean started leaving home without telling his foster mother where he was going. The foster mother continued to say she was committed to working with Sean and even considered becoming his legal guardian.

However, there were continuing concerns with Sean's behavior and the social worker had concerns about the capacity of the foster parents to provide a permanent home for Sean. Twenty-two months into the case, the Foster Family Agency (FFA) social worker submitted a seven-day notice for the home, but the foster mother repeated she wanted to keep Sean. Sean spent a short period of time in a respite foster home but was returned to this foster home by the end of the case record review.

Case notes reflected the social worker's ongoing concerns about how Sean's behavior consistently disrupted his placements and undermined his emotional stability. Sean continued to struggle academically and received multiple detentions and suspensions. He was arrested on two separate occasions for pretending a BB-gun he was carrying was real and for damaging property in a neighbor's garage

Four months after removal, Sean's psychological evaluation was completed. The evaluator diagnosed Sean with attachment disorder inhibited type, depressive disorder not otherwise specified, and ADHD. A medical evaluation was recommended to determine an appropriate course of treatment. The social worker discussed with Sean's therapist the pros and cons of his current placement. Sean had been integrated into the family, he was connected to two children in the home, the foster mother could work with the Sean's behaviors, and he got along with the foster father. However, the foster mother especially felt more comfortable speaking Spanish and Sean was often confused because he did not understand and could not communicate with his foster parents fully. Sean's social worker indicated in case notes, that she did not feel this home could be recommended as a long-term placement because the foster parent's primary language was Spanish and Sean's was English.

The social worker and Sean's therapist met with Sean and foster parents in the foster home. Both Sean and foster parents had placement concerns. Sean stated the language barrier was still an issue and he no longer liked the school he was attending. He stated he did not like being in the foster home, so he had started spending a few nights a week with friends and weekends with family. The foster parents stated Sean had started being disrespectful, was late to school and not doing well, and he was coming home late or not at all. The social worker made suggestions about how they could work together on these issues. One week later, the foster parents gave a seven-day notice, and however the FFA social worker told the social worker she wanted the placement to be salvaged. The FFA social worker cited ongoing communication problems as the reason for the notice.

A team meeting was held including Sean who actively participated, according to case notes. No placement could be found near Sean's current or former school. A potential home with no other children was found and a pre-placement meeting was set up. The following day, it was discovered the home was no longer available because another child had been placed there. It was agreed Sean would go on an extended visit with his maternal aunt and would be assigned to independent studies to keep up with his school assignments. Three days later, Sean was taken to a pre-placement interview with a potential foster home.

One month after the team meeting, Sean was placed in a new foster home. The social worker met with Sean the following day and case notes reflect he was engaged and laughing during the meeting. Sean was regularly visiting his mother, maternal aunt, cousins, and siblings. Visits were also arranged with a maternal cousin who lived nearby. The cousin had a 6-month-old baby and a 10-year-old son and stated she was not able to take Sean in at this time, but she was happy to have him visit during the day.

Although Sean had lived with his maternal aunt and wanted to return to her care, she never applied to be a placement for her nephew. Case notes were unclear about communication between the social worker and Sean's aunt regarding providing a home for Sean. Sean visited regularly with other maternal relatives during the time under review but none expressed willingness to accept him in their homes.

COURT PROCEEDINGS

Jurisdiction/Disposition Hearing

The juvenile court determined sufficient evidence had been presented by the agency to find that Sean had been neglected and abandoned by his parents and found Sean to be a dependent of the court. The social worker recommended reunification for both parents. The parents stipulated to the findings and recommendations. The case plan was for Sean to return home with the anticipated date as the six-month status review hearing.

The mother's case plan centered on her parenting skills and demonstrating willingness to have Sean in her care and parent him. The mother told the social worker she was still not willing to have Sean in her home. The mother's service plan required her to show the ability and willingness to have custody of her child; meet her child's physical, emotional, medical, and educational needs; demonstrate knowledge of age appropriate behavior as applied to her child; consistently, appropriately, and adequately parent her child; and show ability to understand her child's feelings and give emotional support. Sean's mother was required to participate in family and individual therapy (a minimum of eight sessions) including addressing her attachment issues with Sean, her own childhood traumas, and her current difficulties as a single parent. She was also required to fully participate in and successfully complete a parenting series.

Sean's father's service objectives were largely the same with the added requirement that he stay free from illegal drugs, drug test as required, and abide by the law and avoid being arrested. He was required to participate in family counseling and complete a parent education program consisting of a minimum of 12 sessions. He was also required to regularly contact the social worker.

Sean's plan centered on his cooperation with his placement and his social worker, as well as his educational needs. Sean was given individual counseling as well as education support.

Six-Month Status Review Hearing

The social worker recommended in the report to the court that reunification services be continued for both parents, and Sean's case plan goal remained return home. The social worker reported that Sean had been staying with his mother every other weekend for overnight visits for the past four weeks and with his maternal aunt for overnight visits on the other weekends. This visitation began while he was in his second foster home and resumed when he was placed in his current foster home. The mother stated she wanted to see Sean "do better." The report reflected the first time Sean had told his social worker he wanted to live with his mother.

Sean's mother did not engage in any of the services required by her case plan. There was a period of time when the mother participated in individual counseling, but she started attending for reasons unrelated to Sean. During counseling, the mother acknowledged she was unable to bond with Sean, but according to her counselor, she would not be able to effectively work on this bond because she was unwilling to enter family counseling. Sean and his mother were having frequent weekend visits, but the case notes included little documentation about how the visits went. The visiting continued throughout the case review.

Twelve-Month Status Review Hearing

The social worker's report to the court described the mother's progress on her case plan as minimal with the explanation that she became pregnant during the review period. Eleven months into the case, Sean's mother told her social worker she was pregnant, felt overwhelmed, did not plan to engage in her case plan, and wanted to terminate her parental rights over Sean. A month later, she called the social worker again and stated she had changed her mind and would work on her case plan during her maternity leave. The mother was in individual therapy for a matter unrelated to Sean's case. The family therapist called the social worker to notify her that family therapy had not begun. The social worker asked the therapist to hold off on starting services because the mother was still ambivalent about therapy. The mother did not have regular visits with Sean during this reporting period.

The court report indicated that Sean was comfortable in his school and an Individualized Education Plan (IEP) assessment had been initiated through the social worker. The social worker met with Sean at his school for a team meeting to expedite his assessment for learning disabilities to determine if he qualified for an IEP. Case notes did not indicate which specific learning disabilities were assessed. The social worker attempted to call the mother and maternal aunt to have them participate via phone, without success. Neither case notes nor the court records indicate that the social worker filed a motion to transfer Sean's educational rights from his mother to another person.

The agency recommended terminating reunification services for his mother and maintaining Sean in his current out-of-home placement with the foster family. The plan was for this foster family to be Sean's permanent placement until he reached adulthood. Although Sean had visits with his mother, his siblings, and other relatives during the reporting period, the visits were inconsistent. At the hearing, the mother told the social worker and the court she wanted six more months of reunification services. Reunification services were continued for an additional six months.

Eighteen-Month Status Review Hearing

At the 18-month hearing, the social worker recommended that reunification services be terminated and the mother agreed. Sean's mother remained unwilling to have Sean in her home. A permanent plan of alternate permanent planning living arrangement was approved by the court.

Sean remained in long-term foster care with his foster parents. Sean had improved in school and was receiving 504 supportive services. Instead of being suspended when he acted out in school, his teachers assigned him individual projects. The foster parents had established good communication with his teachers and coordinated in-home support with his behavior in school and projects. Sean reported he felt supported in the foster home and bonded to his foster mother.

A team meeting was scheduled after the review to add supports to his placement. The social worker agreed to apply for in-home behavioral services for the foster parents and a Court Appointed Special Advocate (CASA) volunteer for Sean. Sean's foster mother indicated she had decided she wanted to become Sean's legal guardian. When legal guardianship was presented to Sean, according to the case notes, he appeared indifferent but expressed enthusiasm about adoption. Sean's case plan was amended to long-term foster care with the goal of guardianship.

At the end of the case record, Sean was no longer receiving services from his therapist, the FFA social worker who had established a close relationship with Sean, or the specially assigned permanency support counselor. Each of these providers stopped working with Sean while he was transitioning to a new permanency social worker.

End of case record review.

DISCUSSION QUESTIONS

1. When placing children in foster care, what are the specific criteria that should be followed?
    *   What is the importance of placing children in the same school district?
2. Why is it important for Sean to maintain connections with family members and other adults providing support?
    *   List the losses you can identify in the above case summary.
3. There is mention of sibling visitation in the case summary.
    *   What suggestions do you have to keep Sean connected to his siblings when he does not return home?
    *   Why is this important?
4. It is not unusual for Spanish-speaking children to be placed in non-Spanish-speaking households. Sean is facing similar circumstances.
    *   How can you overcome a language/cultural barrier to help Sean or any child feel more comfortable in placement?
5. What information does Sean share with his foster family and/or his social worker that will help to identify a stable placement?

Lucia R.

Lucia R. is an infant girl removed at birth from her mother due to criminal warrants; efforts to engage her father were questionable, but an eager adoptive home was found

FAMILY CONFIGURATION

Household Members

Lucia: newborn
Mother: age 22
Younger brother: age 1, in placement with active reunification case
Older brother: age 5, adopted previously

INITIAL RISKS AND HARMS

Lucia's mother gave birth to her in a hospital outside the county where she had been living in hopes of not being detected by the child welfare agency. Lucia's mother had two older children who had previously been removed from her by child protective services. Shortly after giving birth to Lucia, the mother was arrested at the hospital on a fugitive warrant for violating the terms of her parole by leaving her drug treatment program.

Lucia was removed from her mother and taken into protective custody. The mother asked that Lucia be placed with Lucia's maternal grandmother or maternal great-aunt. The emergency response social worker confirmed the mother had a history of involvement with child welfare services in the adjacent county and a criminal history, most of which involved drugs and some domestic violence. The mother provided the name of Lucia's biological father and contact information. A criminal records check showed the father had a criminal history, related primarily to drugs as well as some domestic violence incidents involving the mother. The mother said they were no longer living together but he was still living in the city where she lived previously.

Although the mother (and the baby) tested clean at the time of birth for all substances, she admitted she had used methamphetamines and alcohol during her pregnancy. She told the emergency response social worker she had used methamphetamines for about three years but could stop on her own and did not need treatment. She stated she had suffered serious sexual abuse as a child and had been removed from her mother and placed in foster care at 7 years old and then adopted at 11 years old. She acknowledged she sometimes suffered from severe depression which she thought was linked to her substance use and admitted she had never completely committed to therapy or gotten help. She said she was willing to enter residential drug treatment as soon as possible to help her get custody of her daughter.

The social worker did not make contact with the father until paternity testing was arranged, about four months after Lucia was removed from her mother. Case notes indicated that the father's girlfriend had left messages on his behalf explaining the father did not speak English and, as a result, was afraid to reply to messages from the social worker. The social worker continued to try to reach the father through letters written in English with referrals to programs, without identifying those with services for Spanish-speaking parents. Copies of the court reports were not sent to the father until he established his status as Lucia's presumed father, and the court had declined to appoint counsel to represent him due to his failure to appear in court.

FINDING A HOME FOR LUCIA

The mother's first choice was for Lucia to live with her in a residential treatment program. Alternatively, if she could not have her daughter placed with her now, she wanted Lucia to live with her maternal grandmother or maternal great-aunt. The case notes reflect that contact was made only with Lucia's maternal great-aunt, who failed to submit the necessary information to be screened for placement. Other relatives were named but did not respond to the social worker's inquiries regarding providing a placement for Lucia.

Lucia was placed with a foster family within 48 hours of removal. The foster parents expressed their interest in adopting Lucia if she was not reunified with her mother. Case notes reflect that during all casework visits and in all contacts with the foster parents, they consistently expressed their readiness to adopt Lucia. The foster family who had adopted Lucia's five-year-old brother was in communication with her foster parents and expressed their desire to have Lucia and her brother get to know each other and possibly be raised together. Visits were arranged and continued through the end of the case.

For the duration of the case, the social worker described Lucia as a happy baby, content and well-adjusted. Medical reports indicated she was developmentally and emotionally on track.

COURT PROCEEDINGS

Jurisdiction/Disposition Hearing

The child welfare agency filed a petition with the juvenile court alleging that Lucia had been neglected by her mother as a result of the mother's drug use and had been abandoned by her father. The petition asked the court to remove Lucia from her parents and assign her care, custody, and control to the agency. The social worker recommended the mother be bypassed for reunification services based on her prior child welfare history, specifically, that two children had recently been removed from her care and her parental rights had been terminated for one of those children.

The mother's first child had been adopted out of foster care due to general neglect, substance abuse, and caretaker absence. The mother had not complied with her case plan and parental rights were terminated three years previously. Her second child was placed into protective custody three months prior to Lucia's removal, due to caregiver absence. The mother had left him with a neighbor for four months without returning for the child. There was no information about the mother's relationship with this son or her progress on reunification provided to the court in the jurisdiction/disposition report.

The court declined to allow child protection to bypass reunification services for the mother and set an interim review hearing to confirm that the mother had entered the residential drug treatment program and to determine paternity and the father's capacity to parent Lucia. The court stated that due to Lucia being an infant, reunification services would be strictly time limited and the decision to order reunification services would be based on the information provided at the interim hearing. The social worker was required to document the parents' willingness and capacity to provide a safe environment for Lucia and meet her needs. The father was required to establish his status as Lucia's presumed father before the court would order reunification services, and the court required the father affirm his desire to participate in reunification services.

The court report included service objectives and a case plan for both parents. The service objectives for the mother were the following:

- Show your ability and willingness to have custody of your child.
- Obtain resources to meet the needs of your child and to provide a safe home.
- Maintain relationship with your child by following the conditions of the visitation plan.
- Cooperate with services to achieve legal permanency.
- Develop and use a specific domestic violence relapse prevention plan for yourself.
- Stay sober and show your ability to live free from alcohol dependency.

- Stay free from illegal drugs and show your ability to live free from drug dependency. Comply with all required drug tests.
- Meet your child's physical, emotional, medical, and educational needs.
- Follow all conditions of probation/parole.
- Obtain and maintain a stable and suitable residence for yourself and your child.
- Be nurturing and supportive when you visit your child.
- Take appropriate action to avoid being a victim of further domestic violence.
- Comply with medical or psychological treatment.
- Cooperate with staff person(s) to support a long-term placement for the child.

The mother's case plan required her to engage in weekly individual therapy to help her learn ways to handle her depression without using drugs and/or alcohol and to process past traumas. The mother was required to complete both a parenting education course focused on infants and a psychological evaluation through an agency approved provider in order to determine if psychotropic medication would assist in her treatment. Regarding substance abuse treatment, the mother was required to enter an inpatient substance abuse treatment program for a minimum of 6 months, preferably 12 months if possible. The mother was ordered to remain in the program until she graduated or had the approval of the court.

The service objectives for the father were that he attend and demonstrate progress in a county certified 52-week domestic violence prevention plan, establish paternity for Lucia, refrain from abusive or threatening behavior, and complete a parenting education course focused on infants.

Lucia's mother was not immediately able to enter residential treatment. She remained in legal custody for two months until a program in the area could be located. During that time, case notes do not reflect any communication with the social worker or consideration of making arrangements for visitation with Lucia. The first case notes indicating conversations between the social worker and the mother occur after the mother had been in residential treatment for five months. According to treatment staff, the mother had been "making excellent progress." In the program, the mother had been attending parenting classes, participating in individual therapy, and complying with psychotropic medications. Her visits with Lucia were described as "positive." She was said to be nurturing, loving, and affectionate with Lucia and became emotional when Lucia had to leave, saying she "missed" her.

Based on the mother's participation in the treatment program, the social worker filed an interim report with the court requesting that the mother be provided with reunification services. She had completed over five weeks of the program without incident at the time of the interim report. The social worker concluded the mother had demonstrated she was ready and willing to care for her daughter.

Shortly thereafter, the social worker contacted the mother's parole officer to discuss the mother's progress and reunification services. The parole officer stated the mother had left the program at least two times in the past five weeks and returned within a day or two. Her drug tests upon returning to the program were always negative. After consultation with the parole officer, program treatment staff had referred the mother for a psychological evaluation and infant-parent therapy, both of which could be incorporated into her residential treatment program.

Interim Review Hearing

At the interim review hearing, the social worker provided information about the father for the first time. The paternity test had confirmed the alleged father was Lucia's biological father and presumed father. Other than arranging for the paternity testing, the social worker had no contact with the father. The social worker reported mailing referrals for programs including domestic violence and parenting education and monthly letters to the father's address; however, at the time of the interim review hearing, the father had not responded. The court again ordered that the father was not to be offered reunification services until he appeared in court and requested services. No efforts by the social worker to meet with the father were reported.

The mother did not appear at the interim review hearing and her whereabouts were unknown. Neither the program staff nor the social worker had been able to contact her or knew why she had left the program. Attempts to locate the mother through family members were unsuccessful. According to staff at the residential treatment program, the mother had been absent without leave (AWOL) many times over the past two months and was not working on her case plan other than visiting with her daughter.

The agency recommended Lucia remain in out-of-home placement and the mother continue to receive reunification services. The court determined adoption was the appropriate concurrent plan for Lucia. The court declined to order reunification services for the father until he demonstrated his willingness to participate in a case plan.

The following month, the social worker approved supervised visits for Lucia with her father. The father began visiting Lucia two weeks after the interim hearing. The visits were described as going well; the father was attentive and caring with his daughter.

Six-Month Status Review Hearing

At the dependency status review hearing, the social worker recommended that the court continue Lucia as a dependent of the court in out-of-home placement, the mother's reunification services be terminated, and a hearing be set to determine the appropriate permanent plan for Lucia. The social worker recommended parental rights be terminated and Lucia be freed for adoption.

During this time, the mother's whereabouts remained unknown and the court found the agency had demonstrated due diligence in attempting to locate and serve her. The mother's parole officer confirmed that she had an active warrant in an adjacent county. The agency was unable to locate the mother by the end of the case record.

The father had been visiting with Lucia for almost three months at the time of the hearing and had started domestic violence classes. The court's requirement that the father appear in court and request reunification services was not understood by the father. The father's visits with Lucia continued for about four months until they were stopped due to inconsistency. Case notes indicate that the father's inconsistency in visiting with his daughter and missing a few domestic violence classes was due to his work schedule.

At the end of the case review, the court terminated the parental rights of both parents, approved a plan of adoption as Lucia's permanent plan, and appointed Lucia's foster parents to act as her de facto parents.

End of case record review.

DISCUSSION QUESTIONS

1. After reading this case summary, what was your reaction to the information you were provided?
   - Examine your reaction(s).
   - Try to understand why you reacted the way you did.
2. What unanswered questions do you have?
   - How would the answers to these questions be helpful?
3. What are reasonable efforts?
   - Were they met?
   - Explain.
4. With what you know about reunification and the Adoption and Safe Families Act (ASFA), consider how the father was or was not provided services.
   - Putting yourself in the father's shoes, why do you think he responded or did not respond the way he did?
   - If you were the father, what would you have done?
   - What are your thoughts about communication between the social worker and the father?

- What effect might the language barrier have had on the father's ability to play a stronger role in the case's outcome?

5. Lucia was an infant.
   - What do a parent and young child need to create a bond?
   - What kind of visits should be authorized and how often should they occur to create this bond?

6. Why is visitation between Lucia and her mother while her mother is in substance abuse treatment important?

Jayden M.

Jayden M. is a one-year-old girl removed from her mother who was a dependent of the court after reunification with her own mother was unsuccessful

FAMILY CONFIGURATION

Household Members

Jayden: age 1
Mother: age 16, dependent of the court

INITIAL RISKS AND HARMS

Jayden was taken into protective custody from her grandmother's home. Her grandmother called the child welfare agency when Jayden's mother had not returned as promised after the weekend. Jayden's mother had been a dependent of the juvenile court for three years when Jayden was born. Jayden was not made a dependent of the court when she was born but was allowed to live in her mother's care in her foster home. The mother had a history of leaving her placements without permission and returning after a few days or weeks. The social worker contacted Jayden's mother and attempted to explain that Jayden could also become a dependent of the court if the mother did not commit to her care. Jayden's mother was described in the case notes as being hostile and non-cooperative and ended the call.

Jayden's father was incarcerated in a state prison for committing armed robbery.

FINDING A HOME FOR JAYDEN

Jayden was taken to an emergency foster home. Jayden did not show any evidence of physical abuse and adjusted to the move. However, two days after Jayden was placed, the foster parent notified the social worker that another placement would have to be found "because the baby was intimidating" to her cat. The placement social worker had also indicated in the case notes concerns about the adequacy of accommodations for Jayden, specifically, that the foster parent did not have a crib or sleeping area for a baby.

Immediately after the emergency placement, a team meeting was held in which Jayden's maternal grandparents, paternal grandmother, and paternal aunt, and the mother's stepmother participated. It was agreed that the agency would conduct home assessments of all family members and fictive kin who were willing to be a placement for Jayden. The whereabouts of Jayden's mother continued to be unknown, although she started calling the social worker after Jayden was removed, sometimes threatening to "beat her up."

Initial efforts at placement with fictive kin were unsuccessful due to multiple problems with the homes, including inadequate sleeping space, need for structural repairs, and physical conditions that were dangerous to a small child.

The non-related extended family member whom the mother had been placed with contacted the social worker and offered to take care of Jayden. Jayden's mother had returned to the foster home at this point and met with the social worker. She agreed to resume care of her daughter with family maintenance services. Two weeks after Jayden was placed in the foster home, the mother went AWOL.

Jayden remained in this placement until the paternal grandmother threatened the foster mother with a box cutter and brass knuckles during a team meeting held to discuss communication with family members. This was the first of several incidents during the case involving physical threats from family members directed at Jayden's substitute caregivers or other family members.

Jayden was removed and placed in the home of another non-related extended family member. The foster mother reported Jayden initially had trouble adjusting to the new placement. She did not smile or babble and often had night terrors. Case notes of conversations with the foster parent show Jayden continued to wake up in the middle of the night screaming as if she were in pain, at least two times a week. The foster mother remained committed to Jayden and reported that her other behaviors were developmentally on track.

Eight months after Jayden was removed from her mother, Jayden's paternal aunt was assessed for placement. Due to the many transitions and changing caregivers that Jayden had experienced, the transition was carried out slowly, and the social worker, aunt, and foster parent worked together to carefully monitor Jayden's reaction to being introduced to a new person. A therapeutic visitation provider was assigned to assess Jayden's interaction with the aunt during visits. It was agreed that if the paternal aunt completed all scheduled visits and Jayden appeared comfortable with her without consequences after the visit, Jayden would be placed with her aunt.

Four months later, Jayden was moved to her paternal aunt's home and, according to case notes, adjusted well. The paternal aunt told the social worker that she felt she could work with the mother to schedule visits at her home. The aunt expressed she wanted to help Jayden's mother build a foundation for herself and build her relationship with Jayden as well. Initial efforts to establish a visiting schedule were unsuccessful when the mother did not appear for the visits. The aunt requested the social worker's help to establish a written schedule of weekend visits. The social worker agreed to put the new schedule in writing and provide the mother with public transit vouchers. After four weekends with no visits, the aunt reported to the social worker that she had been receiving text messages from the mother with threatening comments and calls from the mother's sister as well. The aunt informed the social worker she planned to contact a lawyer regarding obtaining a restraining order. The aunt agreed to bring Jayden for visits with her mother at the visitation center.

To accommodate her work schedule, the aunt found a nearby daycare for Jayden. An early childhood development assessment of Jayden showed she was on target developmentally and was doing well with other children in daycare. The social worker obtained an order from the court transferring the educational rights for Jayden from her mother to the paternal aunt, giving her authority to make the necessary decisions about Jayden's educational and developmental needs. Until the parents' reunification services were terminated, the paternal aunt worked diligently to support visitation between Jayden and her mother.

COURT PROCEEDINGS

Jurisdiction/Disposition Hearing

At the jurisdiction/disposition hearing, the child protection agency recommended that the court sustain the petition against the mother for general neglect and parental abandonment based on the mother's inability to care for her daughter and provide basic necessities for her. The social worker recommended that the mother receive family maintenance services if she remained in the placement with Jayden. However, if the mother left the foster home, she was prohibited by the court from taking Jayden with her. The court ordered the social worker to file a supplemental petition if the mother left her placement. Jayden's mother did not appear at the hearing.

Jayden's father was incarcerated in state prison serving a sentence for armed robbery. His attorney asked for a continuance to allow the father to appear in court. The court indicated reunification services would be ordered if the father established his status as Jayden's presumed father. The jurisdiction/disposition hearing was continued 90 days for the father to appear in court.

The court report provided a detailed analysis of the mother's history involving child protection. Jayden's mother had been a dependent of the juvenile court for three years, during which she had a history of running away from her placements. Jayden's maternal grandmother had failed to engage in services to reunify with Jayden's mother. According to the mother's social worker, the mother had not been participating in her own case plan, including individual counseling and parenting classes. Therapists' reports indicated that Jayden's mother might have developmental delays, possibly linked to previous experiences of trauma or abuse. Immediately before Jayden had been removed, the mother's social worker had described the mother as exhibiting significant symptoms of paranoia. A treatment plan had not been completed for the mother due to her unwillingness to participate in counseling consistently as well as her AWOLs. There were initial concerns about the mother's use of drugs; however, the mother provided three clean drug tests and the substance abuse treatment requirement was removed from her case plan. The court report also referenced information received from different sources that Jayden's mother may have been sexually exploited, but no related service referrals were documented. According to the maternal grandmother, Jayden's mother was pregnant.

Jayden's mother was described as being bonded to her daughter but not demonstrating basic parenting skills. The mother would often leave Jayden with unrelated people to care for her for days without providing them with infant care necessities. The agency was also concerned that Jayden's mother did not protect her from exposure to violence. It was reported by family members that the mother regularly become violent and out of control in front of Jayden and that violent arguments between the mother and father sometimes involved the use of weapons by both.

The social worker recommended a case plan for the mother specifying service objectives related to parenting and cooperating with her social worker and care provider to resolve problems. She was required to participate in counseling, engage in a psychiatric evaluation and psychotropic medication evaluation and monitoring, and participate in substance abuse treatment and testing as required. The mother's strengths were identified as having extended family/friend support, being physically healthy, and being a good parent who was bonded with her daughter.

Regarding visits, the mother had not visited since Jayden was placed in the third foster home, although the placement was with a non-related extended family member. The social worker described multiple conversations with the mother encouraging the mother to visit Jayden. The mother did not appear to understand why Jayden had been removed from her and repeatedly told the social worker she wanted extended visits and wanted to have Jayden returned so they could be a family. The mother told the social worker she wanted to visit with Jayden in her mother's home and was angry at her mother because she refused to allow her to visit in her home. (The maternal grandmother explained she did not feel safe due to prior threats.) The mother contacted the foster parent and said she would not visit according to her schedule and to "forget it, I'll just have another baby." The foster parent reported to the social worker that, in a recent conversation, Jayden's mother had called her asking her to let her pick up Jayden and indicating they would leave the county. Jayden's mother also told the foster mother that the social worker was not helping her and she was planning to ask for a replacement.

Upon receiving this information from the foster parent, the social worker contacted the mother's attorney and expressed concerns about the mother's expressed intention to flee with Jayden and not engage in services. The mother's social worker also spoke to Jayden's social worker about the mother's ability to parent Jayden. The mother's social worker indicated she would be referring the mother to an emancipation program and believed the mother could not complete any part of her case plan.

During the continuance of the jurisdiction/disposition hearing, the mother began visiting with Jayden. Visitation notes described Jayden as bonded to her mother but described the mother as having inappropriate age expectations and being frustrated when Jayden could not respond. The social worker reminded the mother that if she continued to visit regularly, the visits could become unsupervised and increased to multiple hours, to a full day, and then to weekends.

At the continued disposition hearing, the court declared Jayden to be a dependent of the court, removed Jayden from her parents, and ordered her to be placed in foster care. Family reunification services were recommended and ordered for both parents. The court advised the parents that due to Jayden being under three years of age, reunification services were time limited by statute.

Six-Month Status Review Hearing

The court report summarized the case activity during the prior six months, including the mother's progress on her case plan, visiting, Jayden's placement, and information from providers working with Jayden and mother. The mother's progress on her service objectives was rated as "not determinable." The report acknowledged various obstacles that had impacted the mother's ability to work on her case plan and service objectives. The mother had experienced several different placements during the case and would often leave her placement without notifying Jayden's social worker. For a few weeks, the mother could not be reached and her whereabouts were unknown. She also engaged in several violent incidents with her own caregivers which disrupted her placements. One caregiver contacted the social worker after the mother had to be stopped from taking a knife to someone's car, and told the social worker the mother should be "locked up in a psych ward."

The mother's frequent moves and placement changes made it difficult for her to engage in services and visit Jayden. Some of the mother's placements were much further away from Jayden's foster home, and the mother gave that as the reason for not visiting regularly. Visitation was inconsistent throughout the case, including consecutive weeks without any visits. Placement changes also required the social worker to locate and authorize new service referrals in different locations. It was particularly challenging to help the mother establish a therapeutic relationship, fully engage with mental health services, or build a rapport with a therapist. During periods when Jayden's mother was able to attend therapy regularly, her placement was sometimes changed because she acted out or ran from placement, or due to the unwillingness of the foster parents to keep her.

After the six-month review, the agency recommended termination of family reunification services and a permanent plan of legal guardianship with the paternal aunt who was Jayden's current placement. Jayden's mother objected to these recommendations. The court ordered an additional six months of reunification services based on the mother's arguments that Jayden was bonded to her, the mother's placements had changed making it more difficult to maintain a visiting schedule, and she had few visits over the past eight weeks.

Twelve-Month Status Review Hearing

Between the 6-month status review and the 12-month permanency hearing, the mother continued the same pattern of behavior and visitation as during the early months after Jayden was removed.

The mother's mental health status emerged as a concern towards the end of the case record. The mother was placed on a temporary involuntary psychiatric hold after an altercation at the assessment center where she was temporarily placed awaiting a new placement. The mother came into the center asking to call her "pimp" and was attempting to recruit other girls. The staff members were unable to deescalate her and the mother pulled a phone off the wall. She was held in an inpatient psychiatric unit for five days and was discharged back to the assessment center. The mother refused to reveal her diagnosis to her social worker.

Two months after the hearing, the mother called Jayden's social worker and informed her that she had moved, would like all services transferred to where she was living, and requested more visits. The service provider from the visitation center reported to the social worker that visits had been going well and the mother was now living with her stepmother, who had been a previous placement. The social worker contacted the stepmother who reported the mother had not returned from visiting, although she had provided her with a public transit ticket.

A team meeting was scheduled to coincide with the mother's visiting day. The mother did not appear at the meeting but called the social worker during the meeting, stating that she was upset, wanted her baby returned to her, and did not understand why Jayden had been removed. She stated that she was working on locating independent housing and planned to stay with her stepmother until she found housing for herself and Jayden. She stated she would be 18 in two months and would be graduating from high school. The mother's therapist reported that the mother had attended her initial assessment but had not attended weekly sessions. The therapist stated she needed to meet with the mother two more times to develop a treatment plan.

The following month, the social worker spoke again with the mother's therapist. The therapist voiced she felt certain things were "lost in translation" in attempting to communicate with the mother. A formal treatment plan had not been established for the mother, but several concerning symptoms of declining mental health were noted (i.e., preoccupation and excessive worry and difficulty concentrating and completing sentences). The therapist recommended a medication evaluation, a referral for an adult development assessment, trauma-focused intervention, and regular therapy. The therapist also shared that she attempted to engage the mother in a conversation about missed visits and accountability. The mother became upset and escalated the conversation and stated she did not need any help. The therapist said she planned to contact the mother later in the week but would be leaving the program and the mother's case would be transferred to another therapist.

The visitation clinician expressed concerns to the social worker about the relationship between Jayden and her mother. The mother had only met with Jayden for 5 of the 16 scheduled therapeutic sessions. During those visits, the mother appeared to be in her own world and would gently hit Jayden when Jayden hit her. The clinician expressed the opinion that it was difficult for the mother to understand things from her child's perspective and seemed to be making little progress in her parenting. It was recommended therapeutic visitation sessions be decreased from once a week to once a month.

After the conversation with the mother's therapist, the social worker reached the mother. She said she was following her case plan and wanted Jayden back. The social worker explained if she did not visit Jayden regularly, reunification would not take place, and that in order to have more visits, she would have to start visiting regularly. The following week, the mother left a message for the social worker that she was living with her mother and was no longer interested in case plan services.

The social worker recommended that reunification services be terminated and the permanency plan for Jayden be changed from return home to guardianship with her paternal aunt. The paternal aunt told the court she was open to adopting Jayden; however, she stated that Jayden's parents were still young and she wanted them to have an opportunity to change and become better parents in the future.

The court found that the causes necessitating out-of-home placement had not been alleviated, that there was not a substantial probability Jayden could be returned to her mother, and that doing so was contrary to her welfare even if the mother were given additional services. A hearing to terminate parental rights and establish legal guardianship as Jayden's permanent plan was calendared.

End of case record review.

DISCUSSION QUESTIONS

1. What do you know about the difference between guardianship and adoption?
   - Which would you recommend for Jayden and why?
2. How might Jayden's relationship be maintained with her mother after guardianship is finalized?

3. What treatment options or services should be explored for the mother now that you know there may be some signs of her being a victim of exploitation (Commercially Sexually Exploited Children (CSEC))?

4. Thinking about your current strengths, if you were a new social worker working with the mother, what more do you think you could do to engage with her?

    • How do you think she might react and what would you do next?

5. If Jayden is developmentally on target, name three things that might be developmentally appropriate at this time.

    • How would you assess Jayden for each developmental milestone?

6. How does a change in therapist impact services?

    • How does it impact the person participating in therapy?

7. Visitation was not consistent at times.

    • How might consistent visitation have affected the outcome and/or the relationships of the family members?

Caleb D.

Caleb D. is an infant boy living with his 11-month-old sister and parents; parents have a history of substance use and mental health issues; voluntary in-home maintenance with supports is not successful

FAMILY CONFIGURATION

Household Members

Caleb: age 1 month
Mother: age 23
Father: age 25
Older sister: age 11 months, in placement with relatives

INITIAL RISKS AND HARMS

When Caleb was born, a report of neglect or abuse was made to the child welfare agency. The initial follow-up call from the agency failed to produce any information about who made the report or exactly what the reporter had observed that was considered to be child neglect. The agency was familiar with the parents because there was an open child protection case for Caleb's sister and the parents were receiving reunification services. The sister had been placed in the home of her great-uncle and great-aunt. Three weeks after the report regarding Caleb was received, a social worker from the agency made an unannounced visit at the family home. The social worker noted the apartment was "a mess" including dirty dishes, dirty laundry, and spoiled food in the refrigerator. Caleb appeared to be in good health with some dry skin and his crib was clean according to the case notes. The case notes reflected that the parents were instructed to make sure their cat did not sleep near the baby.

A team meeting was held three days later to review the case and complete the risk and safety assessment. At the second visit (which was announced), the mother reported that they had "gotten rid of" the cat due to the social worker's concerns and the apartment had been cleaned. The decision following the meeting was to elevate the referral for Caleb to voluntary family maintenance. Despite the reunification services that were already being provided, the parents appeared to

93

be unable to provide adequate shelter and medical care. In addition, the mother's substance abuse issues interfered with her caring for Caleb. According to the case notes, the father acknowledged that he had a substance abuse problem and although the mother struggled to care for Caleb, he relied on her to be Caleb's primary caregiver.

The mother and father signed a voluntary family maintenance agreement at a meeting at the child welfare agency. The family maintenance case plan stated that two social workers from a family support agency would come to the home seven days a week to provide parenting support. The mother's case plan included following up with a psychiatrist for medication management. The parents also agreed to attend Narcotics Anonymous (NA) meetings and drug test after they completed an outpatient substance abuse program. Caleb's mother had been seeing a therapist for treatment of her chronic depression, bipolar disorder, and anxiety. She was also receiving medication for bipolar disorder. The therapist had previously reported she did not find any issues affecting her capacity or ability to parent and had transferred the mother to another therapist for couples' counseling with the father.

Three weeks later, the mother told the support agency social worker that she had stopped attending therapy and was not taking her psychotropic medication. The mother was directed to complete a new psychiatric assessment. She reported to the social worker that she had previously completed a psychiatric diagnosis and assessment with a psychiatric nurse. Two months later, the social worker was still unable to verify this assessment. When the social worker reached the mother's therapist, she was informed that the psychiatric nurse who completed the assessment was no longer employed at the clinic. The mother no longer had her prescribing psychiatric doctor's contact information and, according to the case notes, the social worker was unable to locate the doctor.

The state disability agency support aide who had been working with the mother reported to the social worker that the parents continued to run out of food and diapers every month despite being provided with these items. She also reported that the lights were often not on in the apartment and it was dirty. She stated that she regularly encouraged the father to find a job but the mother had been discouraging him from getting a job because she was worried he would cheat on her, which according to the mother, he had done in the past.

During an unannounced home visit, the social worker found plastic shopping bags on the apartment floor, clothes on the floor and bed, and choking hazards such as a tag and bottle cap on the floor. The social worker explained to the parents that these were choking and fire hazards. According to the case notes, the parents responded that they did not have time to clean up and that Caleb's sister would make a mess when she was at their home for visitation. After multiple team meetings, it was determined Caleb's parents were unable or unwilling at this time to provide a safe and nurturing environment for Caleb.

FINDING A HOME FOR CALEB

Caleb was placed in his paternal great-aunt and great-uncle's house where his older sister had been placed two months previously. When placement options were researched for Caleb's sister, most relatives who were located were unwilling or unable to provide a placement. The mother objected to placement with her mother because she "did not trust her." Case notes do not indicate any efforts in the search for a placement for Caleb to identify other relatives or non-related extended family members who might be willing, with the exception of the paternal grandmother. The parents agreed to placement for Caleb as well as his sister with the father's great-aunt and great-uncle despite concerns about their health. The aunt had cancer and was in remission and the uncle suffered from dementia.

The social worker expressed continuing concerns in case notes about how these caregivers would be able to care for Caleb and his sister in the short and long term given these health challenges. In addition, case notes reflected ongoing concerns about their judgment and their ability to keep the children safe, including allowing the children to be cared for by their paternal grandmother without permission and taking the children for visits with their parents without prior approval.

COURT PROCEEDINGS

Jurisdiction/Disposition Hearing

The social worker recommended in the jurisdiction/disposition report that the court find the allegations of general neglect against the parents to be true and order that Caleb be removed from their care and placed under the care, custody, and control of protective services, with placement in the home of his great-aunt and great-uncle.

The court report identified the combined substance abuse and mental health history of the parents as the primary factors making this home unsafe for Caleb. Both parents had a history of substance abuse and were receiving outpatient care as part of their family reunification services for Caleb's sister when Caleb was removed from their care. Prior to the opening of Caleb's case, both parents had recently completed inpatient substance abuse programs. Their voluntary family maintenance case plans had required them to attend weekly NA meetings and complete weekly drug tests. The court report did not reference assessments or information from third party service providers regarding the nature of the parents' substance abuse. The mother had been testing regularly for alcohol and illegal drugs; all the tests had been negative and this service objective was reported as met.

In addition, Caleb's mother had a history of mental health problems including depression and bipolar disorder. She received psychiatric treatment during her pregnancy but stopped after the pregnancy. As part of her initial voluntary family maintenance case plan, she had been required to cooperate with the directions of her psychiatric care provider regarding medication, including taking prescribed medications as directed.

The report indicated that the mother had difficulty working with support from the other agencies which had been assigned to her due to her disability. During the prior month, the in-home aide from the state disability agency informed the social worker that the mother's services were being discontinued due to her non-participation. The home was still very dirty at the last visit and the service objective of providing a safe, suitable, and stable home had not been met.

The social worker reported that she had contacted the mother, who explained she was not receiving the help she needed. She said she wanted to "fire" her independent living skills social worker but her provider would not pay for anyone else. The mother explained that she had not been going to therapy because her social workers from the independent living skills agency could not take her. She also accused a worker from that agency of hiding a check from her. (Her Supplemental Security Income (SSI) benefits decreased during this time and she blamed that agency.)

The court approved the recommended case plan for each parent. The service objectives and the case plan elements generally mirrored the needs and services identified in the voluntary family maintenance plan. The mother's case plan required that she complete a mental health assessment approved by the social worker and follow all recommendations, including for psychotropic medications. The mother was required to begin individual counseling, enroll in substance abuse treatment, and develop a "domestic violence relapse prevention plan." The father's case plan was similar, with the exception of the mental health requirement, and included the requirement he "attend and demonstrate progress in a County Certified Domestic Violence Prevention Plan." Neither the court report nor case notes described instances of domestic violence between the mother and the father.

The court ordered that Caleb's parents be offered six months of family reunification services. The court reminded the parents that due to Caleb being under three years of age, these services were strictly time limited and that their parental rights would be terminated and Caleb could be adopted or placed in guardianship if they were not making substantial progress in their case plans.

Six-Month Status Review Hearing

At the status review hearing, the social worker recommended that the court order reunification services be terminated for both parents. The parents had not made substantial progress in their case plans, and there was not a substantial likelihood Caleb would be returned to their care within six months.

The court report summarized the parents' activity on their case plans during the prior six months. The mother continued to test clean for drugs and alcohol, although she did not test regularly or as directed. She had not enrolled or participated in a domestic violence prevention program or her parenting class. Despite being referred to therapy twice since being ordered reunification services, she had not begun therapy and had not participated in a psychiatric assessment. The only area in which the parents were making progress towards remediating the circumstances that led to Caleb's removal from their home related to seeking employment. Caleb's father was working at an auto parts store and his mother had successfully enrolled in cosmetology school.

The social worker recommended that a selection and implementation hearing be set to identify adoption as the permanent plan for Caleb. The social workers recommended that the current caregivers not be considered as an adoptive home.

End of case record review.

DISCUSSION QUESTIONS

1. What questions would you ask and what information would you need to know to maintain Caleb in the home?
    - What safety planning might you do if Caleb were to stay in the home?
2. The case record notes that the mother reported having trouble with mental health services.
    - Describe what might have been a lack of follow through by the mental health agency or on the part of the social worker.
    - What could you do to prevent this from happening?
    - What would you do if this case had been transferred to you from another social worker who is not in your unit but is still with the county?
3. This case has just been transferred to you from a social worker who is no longer with the agency. You observe in the case plan that there are services for both parents to address domestic violence. In looking at other documents in the file, you do not find any information to support this case plan requirement.
    - Whom would you contact to find if there has been law enforcement involvement?
    - How would you follow up with the parents to find out what may have happened?
4. Consider concurrent planning, and discuss concerns you might have about the paternal great-aunt and great-uncle as a concurrent placement.
    - What safety plans could you put into place?
    - Where would you go from here in regard to concurrent planning?
5. With the Adoption and Safe Families Act (ASFA) in mind, discuss the important timelines and Caleb's age.

Anthony R.

Anthony R. is an 11-year-old boy who grew up in a family where abusive behavior by the father and domestic violence were common

FAMILY CONFIGURATION

Household Members

Anthony: age 11
Mother: age 41
Father: age 56

INITIAL RISKS AND HARMS

When Anthony arrived at school with marks on his face and bruising, he was sent to the school social worker who immediately contacted the child welfare agency. Anthony told the nurse his father hit him the night before when his father came home drunk and began abusing the family dogs. Anthony tried to intervene and protect the dogs and his father punched him once in the face with a closed fist and twice in the ribs. Anthony said his mother was very upset and told him to stay away from his father and not get in the middle. Later, Anthony said his mother helped him clean up.

When interviewed by the police, the mother explained that Anthony and his father were "roughhousing" and Anthony accidentally got hurt. Later, when being interviewed by the assigned social worker, she stated that she was in the kitchen and had not witnessed the incident first hand.

The investigation by the emergency response social worker included statements taken by the reporting police officers and the school social worker. During their interview, Anthony volunteered that his father "likes" hitting him and that he was scared to go home. Anthony said that last year, his father hit him every day. While being interviewed by a school social worker Anthony reported that his father was often aggressive towards him but that last night was the first time his father had punched him with a closed fist in the face. Anthony explained the scars on his hands were caused by his father "teasing to cut him with a knife and then actually causing cuts on his fingers."

The family had a history with child protective services that began shortly after Anthony was born. The family had been referred on five separate occasions for physical abuse and/or general neglect; none of the referrals had resulted in Anthony being removed from his parents. All the referrals involved the father and/or the mother being physically abusive towards Anthony or the father engaging in domestic violence with the mother in front of Anthony. As a result of these incidents, the mother had agreed to a safety plan committing to protect Anthony from physical harm and promising she would take him to a safe place and call the police if the father tried to physically punish him. Anthony's father refused to sign a safety plan because, according to the case notes, he was "not willing to take advice from a 26-year-old girl who had no children and did not know what it was like to deal with real-life situations."

The prior investigations had concluded that the father was the aggressor in physical domestic disputes and was particularly violent when under the influence of alcohol. After Anthony reached elementary school, the abuse was directed toward him as well as his mother, either personally or indirectly, and the mother either failed or was unable to protect him from his father.

In this investigation and all prior investigations, the mother consistently asserted she loved her son deeply and would do anything for him, including leaving the father. The mother described the father as regularly violent and emotionally abusive, particularly when he was under the influence of alcohol. However, she later refused to separate from the father and repeatedly protected him by substantiating his stories and downplaying his physical and emotional abuse towards both herself and her son. According to others who were interviewed, the father had a long history of being controlling and violent towards the mother, including periods when he did not allow her to leave the house without him for any reason.

The case record described the parents as having a tumultuous history for over 16 years as a couple. During those years, the father had assaulted the mother resulting in a restraining order against the father. After the order expired, the father, according to the mother, moved back into her home without her permission. They eventually married (the record does not indicate when) and continued to have a volatile relationship. When Anthony was five years old, the father filed for a separation and the mother asked for a divorce. Their marriage was dissolved, but the couple remained together after their divorce. Three years before the current incident, the mother filed for a domestic violence restraining order against the father but, according to the mother, the father "could not be served" and the order was not issued.

During the father's meeting with the emergency response worker after Anthony was removed, the father described himself as an ex-marine who was "used to functioning at a highly aggressive level." The father had a criminal history for inflicting corporal injury on a spouse, spousal battery, willful cruelty to a child, vandalism, assault with a deadly weapon, battery on a police officer, and possession of narcotics. Anthony's mother had one incident involving threatening with intent to terrorize, spousal battery, and exhibiting a non-firearm deadly weapon. After Anthony was removed from his parents and he was ordered detained by the court, the assigned social worker interviewed the parents. The father explained to the social worker that he was an ex-marine and had been teaching Anthony self-defense to protect him from bullying. The father said that he yells at Anthony when he misbehaves and he is rough with him because he loves him. Regarding the incident causing Anthony to be removed from the parents, the father stated he had a "couple" of beers while watching a game and then came home. He said one of the dogs was running at him so he slapped him on the head to keep him from biting anyone. He also said Anthony jumped on his back and he elbowed him in the stomach to get him off and he was unaware of Anthony's mouth injury and did not intend to hurt him. The father also admitted he once accidentally cut Anthony with a knife when they were playing around. Regarding his relationship with Anthony's mother, he stated they argue "like others."

In her initial interview with the assigned social worker, the mother first stated that she wanted to stay with the father and knew he did not intentionally hurt Anthony. A few minutes later she repeated what she had told the emergency response worker (i.e., that she was willing to move out of the home and would do whatever it took to regain custody of Anthony). The social worker referred the mother to a domestic violence center for help with her decision.

When the mother was interviewed about the father hitting Anthony, she explained that Anthony's father used to be violent towards her but recently stopped. When confronted with Anthony's statements suggesting that the father continued to act violently towards her and had hit her in the face, bruising her eye, as recently as the prior week, the mother claimed the injury was the result of irritated allergies.

The father drank regularly and became more violent towards the mother and Anthony when he was under the influence of alcohol; however, both Anthony and his mother stated that the father would also be violent at times when he was sober. The mother reported that his behavior did not change when he was drinking. She also said he "always" drank and had a demanding and possessive demeanor. Anthony reported that his father was violent with both himself and his mother when he was under the influence of alcohol. He estimated his father drank alcohol once per week and came home drunk once every three months.

FINDING A HOME FOR ANTHONY

The parents agreed to placement for Anthony with relatives, and he was placed in the home of his maternal aunt, uncle, and cousin. Over the next weeks, the aunt and uncle had trouble adjusting to Anthony being in their home. There was also conflict between Anthony and his teenage cousin. Anthony told his lawyer that his aunt and uncle did not help him with homework (he was failing all his classes), his hygiene, or extracurricular activities, "nor did they get him anything for Christmas." The lawyer contacted the social worker who then met with Anthony to discuss his concerns, at which point Anthony said he did not want to be moved. The social worker asked the parents to become more involved in Anthony's education.

One month later, the parents asked the social worker to find another placement for Anthony. After the school semester ended, Anthony was moved to a foster care placement. The case notes do not reflect efforts to identify other relatives who might have been available for placement.

COURT PROCEEDINGS
Jurisdiction/Disposition Hearing

The court found that the allegations of the petition stating that Anthony was abused by his father, and that the father had a history of abusing him and engaging in domestic violence, were true. The court ordered that Anthony become a dependent of the court and remain in out-of-home care. The court further ordered reunification services for both parents.

The court report summarized the circumstances which caused Anthony's removal from his parents, Anthony's injury, the family history and dynamics, and the statements made by the parents and Anthony. The report concluded with the findings of the assessment by the child welfare agency with respect to the family dynamics—namely, that the father did not understand how his behavior affected and/or would affect Anthony, the mother, and others and that the mother was unable to protect her son or herself from the father.

The court report included recommended service objectives for both parents. The service objectives for the mother were the following:

- Maintain a relationship with your child by following the conditions of the visitation plan.
- Protect your child from emotional harm.
- Show that you will not permit others to physically abuse your child.
- Take appropriate action to avoid being a victim of further domestic violence.
- Consistently, appropriately, and adequately parent your child.

The mother's case plan required that she attend and complete a domestic violence program, obtain a restraining order protecting herself from her abuser, participate in therapy and follow provider recommendations, participate in therapy with the child if requested, and complete an approved parenting education program. Regarding supporting Anthony's education, the mother's case plan required that

- She provide Anthony's caregivers with any information needed to help them promote Anthony's success at school;
- Stay in regular contact with his teacher;
- Keep informed about her child's overall progress; and
- Attend all school-based meetings.

The service objectives for the father were the following:

- Maintain a relationship with your child by following the conditions of the visitation plan.
- Be nurturing and supportive when you visit your child.
- Stay sober and show ability to live free from alcohol dependency.
- Interact with your child without physical abuse or harm.
- Do not behave in a manner that is verbally, emotionally, physically, or sexually abusive or threatening.

The father was required in his case plan to complete a domestic violence program, complete an assessment and follow treatment recommendations, participate in therapy and follow provider recommendations, participate in therapy with his child if requested, cooperate with a drug and alcohol assessment and follow treatment recommendations including testing as required, and complete a parenting education program. Like the mother, the father was required to assist in his son's education as appropriate.

The court ordered biweekly visiting between Anthony and his mother. The father was ordered to work with a mental health specialist, and depending on the recommendations of the therapist, the social worker was given the discretion to authorize therapeutic visits between the father and Anthony. All visits were ordered to be supervised.

The following month, the father was sentenced for an earlier domestic violence offense against the mother and was ordered to complete a 52-week domestic violence program.

Six-Month Status Review Hearing

The court report recommended that reunification services be extended six more months to both parents. The service objectives and responsibilities for the parents remained unchanged from the prior case plan and the parents' progress towards their respective service objectives was categorized as not determinable.

The report indicated the social worker had met with the parents after the disposition hearing and provided them with referrals for the programs required by their case plans.

About three months into the case, the father began attending a men's support group for domestic abusers. He participated in this group throughout the life of the case and the group leader reported to the social worker that the father made significant personal progress. The father began the parent education program after the disposition hearing and attended regularly for the first two months. The instructor reported to the social worker that the father attended all the parenting classes but did not score well on his performance because he was argumentative and did not complete homework or participate in class. In his monthly interview with the social worker, the father was unable to explain what he learned from parenting classes.

The father had completed his case plan requirement of cooperating in a drug and alcohol assessment and reported to the social worker that he had been sober for 10 months and was actively participating in Alcoholics Anonymous (AA). The father said he was seeing his therapist "on a regular basis" and had been attending a men's support group for abusers for almost six months. The father had been referred to a life-skills program to help him more effectively deal with daily life and reported to the social worker he was learning useful things.

The father continued to deny being abusive towards Anthony and specifically denied that he intentionally injured Anthony in the incident leading to Anthony's removal. The social worker acknowledged the father's progress, encouraged him to continue, and reminded him that he was required to prove he was not using drugs and had to make an appointment with the substance abuse agency to arrange random drug testing.

At their monthly meeting, the mother told the social worker she had stopped going to her domestic violence program because she has been going for over 10 years, and she claimed someone who worked for the program told her it was time to stop. The social worker shared with the mother information provided by her aunt and uncle that the mother had been a victim of domestic violence for over 12 years, since before Anthony was born. The mother denied having problems with the father over many years and continued to minimize and deny the level of abuse by the father. She claimed to not remember the incident leading to Anthony's removal. The mother reported she was enjoying her parenting classes, attended 22 classes, and would continue attending.

The parents' first contact visit was arranged; the social worker had tried to arrange earlier visits but Anthony refused. The social worker required the parents to report back about the visit. Although both parents reported that the visit went well, Anthony's therapist reported that after the visit Anthony was more guarded and had a depressive mood, mostly irritable. The parents missed their visits with Anthony the next month due to their confusion about the time and location of the visits and the father attending therapy appointments and drug testing despite being told by the social worker that visiting takes priority.

The social worker met with the parents to discuss their visits with Anthony. The visitation supervisor reported that when Anthony behaved poorly, both parents set firm limits with him as they learned in parenting classes. At the visit the following month, Anthony asked parents to bring their dog to the visit and they agreed. At the next visit, they did not bring the dog nor did they bring any food (which they had been instructed to bring with them). The father said hello to Anthony and then did not speak to the mother or Anthony for the duration of the visit. The parents wrote apology letters to Anthony and read the letters to him during the next visit and Anthony accepted their apologies.

The father's therapist had reported that the father had recently acknowledged his parenting strategies were too punitive. The social worker discussed the parenting skills the parents had learned in their classes. Both parents agreed to work more closely with their service providers to apply the skills they were being taught when they visited Anthony.

At the next monthly meeting, the mother refused to meet with the social worker. Anthony's attorney informed the social worker that the father had been encouraging the mother to stop working with the social worker.

Twelve-Month Status Review Hearing

The service objectives and case plan responsibilities for the parents remained unchanged. All objectives were rated as not determinable. For the previous three months, the father had been drug testing with negative results. The mother returned to a women's domestic violence program; one of the mother's service providers reported the mother was making positive progress and Al-Anon was helping her to overcome co-dependency.

The father notified the social worker that he was making progress in AA and had been assigned to work with an AA sponsor. The father's therapist informed the social worker that the father was learning how to set limits with Anthony, how to stop conversations when he is upset and resume them once he is calmer, and to be more specific and less generalized in his communication.

Anthony's attorney contacted the social worker about the increased visitation between Anthony and his parents. The attorney told the social worker that he believed Anthony's father was simply going through the "motions" to get Anthony back but not making, or interested in making, true progress.

The social worker changed visitation to one supervised and two unsupervised visits per week. The parents' case had closed at the parents' visiting center and the center had recommended unsupervised visits. The following month, Anthony told his social worker the visits were going well and he wanted longer, more frequent, and overnight visits. Anthony talked positively to his attorney about seeing his parents, which had not always been the case. The social worker met with the parents to review the safety plan they wrote in case the father relapsed and was under the influence of alcohol. The meeting was followed by Anthony's first overnight visit with his parents. Two weeks later, Anthony began an extended 30-day visit.

The social worker received a report that the father tested positive for marijuana. He later explained he had a medical marijuana card and he smoked because of anxiety and was unaware he was not to be consuming any controlled substances.

Eighteen-Month Status Review Hearing

The court report summarized the progress of the parents with their case plans and especially their progress in establishing a positive relationship with Anthony. The social worker reported that she had been noticing a positive change in how Anthony was interacting with his parents but continued to believe the risk to his well-being remained high due to historical events and the slow initial case progress. As a result, the social worker recommended six more months of reunification services.

Throughout the case, the mother had complied with her case plan and used the tools she learned in parenting and domestic violence classes with Anthony and the father. She expressed commitment to her family and appeared to learn how to prioritize her own and Anthony's well-being. However, concern was expressed by the mother's domestic violence program counselor that she never reported further incidents of domestic violence between herself and the father, and it was unclear if this was because the father's behavior truly changed or if she was trying to protect him.

The mother had accomplished all of her service objectives with the exception of her continuing responsibilities:

- Protect your child from emotional harm.
- Show that you will not permit others to physically abuse your child.
- Take appropriate action to avoid being a victim of further domestic violence.
- Consistently, appropriately, and adequately parent your child.

Regarding her case plan, the mother was required to

- Continue her domestic violence classes;
- Continue to participate in therapy and follow provider recommendations;
- Continue to participate in therapy with the child, if deemed necessary by the therapist; and
- Accept the child's disclosure and support the child for telling the truth in the past and encourage him to do so in the future.

The mother was required to continue supporting her son, his education, and the caregiver while her son is in placement and provide his caregiver with any information to help them promote his success at school.

The father had met some of his service objectives and was rated as in progress on his other service objectives:

- Stay sober and show ability to live free from alcohol dependency.
- Interact with your child without physical abuse or harm.
- Consistently, appropriately, and adequately parent your child.
- Do not behave in a manner that is verbally, emotionally, physically, or sexually abusive or threatening.

The father was required to

- Continue his domestic violence program;
- Continue to participate in therapy and follow provider recommendations;
- Continue to participate in therapy with the child; and
- If deemed necessary by the therapist, accept the child's disclosure and support the child for telling the truth in the past and encourage him to do so in the future.

The social worker petitioned the court to set an interim hearing to consider reunification with family maintenance services. The mother had completed parenting classes and was regularly seeing a therapist. The father was also seeing a therapist weekly and drug testing once per week. He also completed the parenting class and had two remaining classes to complete his 52-week domestic violence program. The father's domestic violence group leader reported the father had shown great personal growth over the past year.

Two months after the family reunified, the father began to express his objections to the social worker meeting with Anthony and his attorney without him being present. Six weeks later, the father's therapist reported to the social worker that although his attendance had been good, the father had demonstrated little progress with respect to changing his desire to control situations involving the mother and/or Anthony. The therapist also reported that the father threatened to fire him weekly and boasted about putting his new social worker in his place.

Six months after reunification, the case notes indicate that the social worker had continuing concerns about the father's understanding of his behavior and unwillingness to take responsibility for abusing his son and the mother. The case notes describe the father as warm and welcoming during scheduled visits with the social worker but as controlling when the social worker attempted to meet with the mother or Anthony without him. The mother had a safety plan in place if the father began to act abusively, and the record noted that the father understood his role in the safety plan and why it was necessary. In conversations with the social worker, the father was still unable to define what step he was working on from the 12-step program but was able to identify 5 triggers of relapse and 3 coping strategies for relapse prevention.

The father never stated that his actions played a role in Anthony's removal from the home. While the case records indicated he developed effective parenting skills and coping mechanisms, his temper and controlling behavior remained present through the end of the case.

Child protective services recommended the family continue to receive family maintenance services. The parents objected. The court ordered the case dismissed.

End of case record review.

DISCUSSION QUESTIONS

1. When looking at the incident with Anthony and his family that brought him into foster care, describe the difference between risk and safety.

2. What information would you need from Anthony's parents in order to assess what they learned from their parenting classes?

3. What protective capacity, if any, do you see in Anthony's mother?
   - What would you like to see her demonstrate?

4. List at least three requirements for a safety plan to protect Anthony from being hurt as a result of domestic violence in his home and/or his father physically abusing him.

5. If you were to arrive at the home and walked in on a physical altercation between the parents, what would you do?

6. What was significant about the social worker asking the father about the 12-step program?

7. What placement information would you like to see in the case summary to determine whether the placement(s) and subsequent moves were appropriate?

Lila S.

Lila S. is a four-year-old girl whose mother was involved in a violent relationship with the father of a younger sibling, leading to removal of both children

FAMILY CONFIGURATION

Household Members

Lila: age 4
Mother: age 24
Younger brother: age 1
Father: father of Lila's brother; not Lila's father, age not specified in case record
Lila's biological father: whereabouts unknown or incarcerated during most of the review

INITIAL RISKS AND HARMS

The child welfare agency's initial contact with this family resulted from the mother being arrested for assault and child endangerment for attempting to run over the father of her son with her car. The father was not injured. Lila and her one-year-old brother were in the car with their mother. The dependency investigations social worker removed the children and began looking for a suitable placement with members of Lila's family. The mother gave the social worker the names of her parents, with whom the family had been living for the prior six months. The maternal grandparents told the social worker they would like the children returned to them where they currently resided with the mother. Both grandparents disclosed criminal arrest histories, which prevented their home from being approved as an emergency placement. Lila's biological father's whereabouts were unknown; according to the grandparents, he had little involvement with her throughout her life. The allegations of caretaker absence and severe neglect were substantiated.

FINDING A HOME FOR LILA

The social worker secured a temporary foster home placement for Lila and her brother while steps were taken to approve the maternal grandparents' home for placement. Both children were then moved from the foster home to the home of the mother's cousin after several days in the temporary placement. The following month, the grandparents' home was approved for placement and Lila and her brother were transferred to their home. The grandparents had registered Lila in kindergarten when the social worker visited. Case notes indicated that Lila appeared happy to be with her grandparents and relaxed in their home. Lila's mother and her brother's father visited the children regularly and case notes indicated the children appeared to be strongly bonded with them. Visits occurred in the grandparents' home.

Three months after the initial hearing, the social worker received the results from Lila's developmental assessment. Lila was found to be on target in all developmental areas, but seemed to be experiencing some residual trauma due to being separated from her mother. During supervised in-home visits with Lila at the grandparents' home, both minors were noted to be doing well in placement, and Lila was looking forward to beginning kindergarten. In a regular visit, Lila told the social worker she did not like it when her mother and her brother's father visited together, because they often argued.

COURT PROCEEDINGS

Jurisdiction/Disposition Hearing

The child protection agency filed a petition with the court alleging parental neglect and abandonment. The petition was sustained by the court and Lila and her brother were made dependents of the court and removed from the custody of her mother. Both fathers were classified as alleged fathers in the absence of proof of paternity. The whereabouts of Lila's father remained unknown at the time. The mother and father of Lila's brother appeared in court and stipulated to the findings. Reunification services were ordered for the mother.

According to the court report, the mother and the children had been living with the maternal grandparents for the prior six months. Lila's grandparents described the mother as having a very volatile relationship with the brother's father and frequently engaging in verbally abusive arguments that at times led to physical altercations. The mother acknowledged multiple reported incidents of domestic violence against the father, some of which Lila directly witnessed. Lila's mother had two prior drug-related arrests three years earlier, which resulted in brief incarcerations when she was unable to care for Lila. The brother's father had a history of arrests for domestic violence and incarcerations for criminal gang-related offenses.

At the time of referral to child protective services, the mother had been in a four-year relationship with the father of Lila's brother. They had lived together previously, but after being evicted, the mother had been forced to move back with Lila's maternal grandparents. According to the mother, she had struggled to obtain employment for years and supported her children with public assistance and the help of her family.

The mother and the father were given case plans containing program requirements and service objectives. The mother's service objectives were the following:

- Show your ability and willingness to have custody of your child(ren).
- Do not involve your child(ren) in attempts to control or intimidate your partner.
- Stay free from illegal drugs and show your ability to live free from drug dependency. Comply with all required drug tests.
- Consistently, appropriately, and adequately parent your child(ren).
- Obtain and maintain a stable and suitable residence for yourself and your child(ren).
- Do not behave in a manner that is verbally, emotionally, physically, or sexually abusive or threatening.

The mother's case plan required her to participate in counseling, specifically couples counseling related to anger and domestic violence; parent education; and substance abuse treatment including random drug testing at the discretion of the social worker.

The case plan for the father's brother included the following service objectives:

- Show your ability and willingness to have custody of your child(ren).
- Stay free from illegal drugs and show your ability to live free from drug dependency. Comply with all required drug tests.
- Do not break the law. Avoid arrests and convictions.
- Show that you know age-appropriate behavior for your child(ren).
- Obtain and maintain a stable and suitable residence for yourself and your child(ren).
- Do not behave in a manner that is verbally, emotionally, physically, or sexually abusive or threatening.

The father's case plan included the same counseling, parent education, and substance abuse treatment requirements as the case plan for Lila's mother. Case notes indicate the father had disagreed with the social worker's recommendations and requested he be given custody of his son. The court ruled that the father needed to demonstrate longer-term stability before Lila's brother could be placed in his care.

Six-Month Status Review Hearing

The social worker's court report summarized the progress the parents had made on their case plan and what needed to be done to reunify. The report noted that the mother was making substantial progress and that the father of Lila's brother was inconsistent in his program participation.

The social worker described the role that family issues, including repeated incarcerations, domestic violence, unstable housing, and inadequate parenting skills, played in the safety of the children and reunification of the parents with Lila and her brother. The social worker noted significant strengths supporting the goal of reunification, including the following: the children were physically healthy, the parents had support from the extended family, and each parent expressed willingness to accept services and work with the social worker.

The social worker described Lila's mother as someone who believed she was a good mother and who needed to secure and maintain a stable home and emotional support in caring for her children as a single mother. The mother acknowledged her need to control her anger and engage in anger management classes.

In face-to-face visits, the social worker talked with the mother about the classes she was attending. The mother reported she was "happy" with the support she was receiving through the anger management and parenting classes. She regularly expressed frustration about obtaining stable housing and described housing as her greatest barrier to completing her case plan objectives and having her children returned to her. Case notes indicate that the mother needed to receive discretionary funds from the child welfare agency because she had found housing and needed assistance with the deposit. The social worker agreed to apply for funds with the mother, as well as refer her to a program that would help her clean up her past criminal record. Although the social worker noticed bruises on the mother's arm, the mother denied any abuse.

The social worker reported that in meetings with the father, he had acknowledged that he and the mother had a toxic relationship, and he said that he would like to learn how to control his anger to avoid being out of control.

The mother failed to appear at the status review, and in the month after the status review hearing, the mother missed a scheduled appointment with her social worker, did not show up twice to an intake for individual therapy, and was not cooperating with the specialized reunification worker. As a result of her failure to participate in these services, the casework support was terminated. Case notes indicated that the social worker supervisor told the social worker she did not believe the mother would be ready to reunify within six months.

The following month, the social worker received a telephone call from the grandfather reporting that he suspected his daughter was being abused. The grandfather reported that when he confronted the brother's father about the bruises on the mother's arm, the father neither confirmed nor denied responsibility. The social worker immediately contacted the mother who admitted having a significant domestic violence history with the father of Lila's brother and acknowledged that Lila had witnessed her mother being abused. The mother also disclosed that the father was involved in criminal activity and might be a trafficker. The social worker and the mother agreed that if she believed she was in danger, she would reach out to the social worker, crisis line, or call the police. The social worker discussed the impact of witnessing or being around domestic violence on Lila and they agreed that Lila and her mother should begin family therapy.

The grandfather subsequently notified the social worker that the mother had to be admitted to the hospital for a broken rib she suffered due to an altercation with the brother's father, but the mother was afraid to contact the police fearing retaliation by the father.

The social worker visited with Lila and her brother at the grandparents' home. Both children appeared to be doing well. Lila said she had just started kindergarten and was having lots of fun. The social worker met privately with the mother and grandfather to discuss the mother's relationship with the father and she stated they had separated. He had been arrested, and she did not plan on seeing him.

Concerns about possible resumed domestic violence arose in subsequent calls from the grandfather. The grandparents were especially concerned about the mother's willingness to take Lila and her brother to visit his father without their knowledge or permission. The social worker met with each of the parents individually to remind them about making progress on their case plan and that statutory requirements could result in the termination of their services and their parental rights if they were not ready to reunify by the permanency hearing in six months.

The social worker met with the grandparents to discuss their concerns and visit the children. The grandfather told the social worker that the father of Lila's brother had "beaten the mother up" and broke multiple of her ribs, which forced her to miss her court hearing. He said the police had witnessed the mother and the father fighting and arrested both at the scene. The social worker contacted the mother who explained that when the police stopped the fight, they discovered he had a restraining order against her. The mother told the social worker the father had given her a bag of heroin. The heroin was found on her at the jail resulting in charges of drug possession, violating a restraining order, and carrying drugs into jail.

The following week when the social worker visited with Lila and her brother, the mother was present and attending to children's needs; both minors appeared well and happy to be with their mother. The mother notified the social worker that her court hearing related to the criminal charges was the following week and she thought the father had left the state.

At the monthly home visit, Lila's grandfather told the social worker that both children were doing very well and family therapy had been going very well. He said he was grateful for the therapist's insights and believed these services had helped their family.

Three weeks later, the grandfather reported to the social worker he was concerned about the mother's well-being. Her mood was very off the last time she visited with the children and, when confronted, she admitted she had been using heroin again. She also told her father she would like to take methadone to help her get off heroin.

In a telephone call with the grandfather, he said that during a recent family therapy session the mother was very distracted and jumpy and was receiving calls and texts throughout the session. He was very concerned that she may be prostituting herself as well. He stressed that multiple family members had attempted to support the mother by offering her housing and employment assistance. The mother stated she was "not ready."

Case notes indicate that Lila's biological father contacted the social worker notifying her he was incarcerated again. The social worker sent a letter to Lila's father reminding him of the open family reunification case and providing him resources and information on how he could make progress on his plan objectives while incarcerated. They had met once while Lila's biological father was on parole. The father had presented proof of enrollment in the 52-week domestic violence offender program. The social worker had provided him with a referral to parenting education classes.

The social worker notified the mother that her case plan was being amended to include hair follicle substance abuse testing and a concurrent plan of adoption. Permanency planning goals were established for the grandparents.

The social worker met with Lila's brother's father at the child welfare offices. He let the social worker know that he had dropped out of his drug program, he and the mother were back together, and he denied domestic violence in their current relationship. He was adamant that he be allowed unsupervised visits with his son, and he urged the social worker to let the family reunify without the interference of child welfare services.

The following day, the grandfather called the social worker reporting that the mother refused to continue with family therapy due to an alleged conflict with the therapist. She also told her father that she had been able to obtain methadone in order to detox.

Twelve-Month Status Review Hearing

At the 12-month status review hearing, the social worker recommended that reunification services be terminated for the mother and both fathers and the court order a permanent plan of legal guardianship for both children with the grandparents. The court report indicated that the parents were incarcerated for criminal trespass; the mother had been testing positive for methamphetamine and marijuana and had stopped attending family counseling. Both parents were still visiting Lila and her brother, but the grandparents reported that they often had to be reminded of the visiting schedule and frequently tried to change scheduled times. Lila told her grandparents and the social worker that she missed her mother and wished she could see her more often. Lila and her brother continued to do well in the grand-parents' home during the social worker visits. The social worker reported that the guardianship paperwork was being completed by the grandparents and should be filed with the court within 30 days.

End of case record review.

DISCUSSION QUESTIONS

1. The case summary states: In the month after the status review hearing, the mother missed a scheduled appointment with her social worker, did not show up twice for an intake for individual therapy, and was not coop-erating with the specialized reunification worker. When parents are "not cooperating," it may be for various reasons other than intentional refusal to participate.
   - What might be reasons/barriers the mother is "not cooperating" other than being unwilling to participate?
   - How might you help her recognize these reasons/barriers?

2. What is your understanding of the need for concurrent planning and how might a permanent plan of adoption versus guardianship be considered?

3. What role does the issue of parental substance use play in this case?
   - Do you see behaviors that are consistent with substance use in the case before it is specifically indicated in the case summary?

4. What factors lead abused individuals to remain with their abusive partners?
   - Do you observe any of these issues or situations with this family?
   - How do you work with the individuals even if they do not separate?

5. As a new worker, you may not have experience working with cases involv-ing domestic violence.
   - Whom might you seek out for assistance or consultation to learn how to engage this family?
   - Why would you reach out to these individuals?

6. What is the importance of a safety plan in this case?
   - What are some important components of this safety plan, keeping in mind not only the mother, but also including the children in the plan?

7. How might you prepare Lila if it became necessary to separate her from her brother permanently?

Brandon B.

Brandon B. is a seven-month-old boy who was removed
from his mother and placed in foster care until his
noncustodial father established his sobriety

FAMILY CONFIGURATION

Household Members

Brandon: age 7 months
Mother: age 34
Older brother: age 8, half-sibling

INITIAL RISKS AND HARMS

Brandon's mother was arrested by city police for driving while under the influence of
alcohol or drugs and driving under the influence with a child on her lap. The child
welfare agency was called and took custody of Brandon. The mother was unable
to provide contact information for Brandon's father or any relatives at the time.

The emergency response social worker was able to locate the father's residence
in a nearby city. He responded promptly to contact and stated that he wanted
Brandon to be placed with him and was willing to do whatever was necessary to
take custody of his son. He had moved to a nearby county and was living with his
parents in order to commute to his job. He told the social worker that he stayed at
Brandon's mother's residence a day or so each week.

At the team meeting on the following day, it was determined that a reference
in the family case file to father having a substance abuse history required that the
father provide proof he was no longer using drugs. The team concluded it would
be in Brandon's best interest to place him in an age-appropriate foster home and
ask the father to begin drug testing.

FINDING A HOME FOR BRANDON

Three weeks after being placed in the foster home, Brandon was placed with his paternal grandparents. The social worker explained to the father and his parents that he could not reside in the home with Brandon. They were all in agreement. Brandon's father was encouraged to regularly visit, but visits were ordered to be supervised.

Two days later, Brandon's grandfather contacted the social worker and stated that he and his wife were not able to care for Brandon at that time. He explained that "the pressure was too much." He was unable to watch Brandon all day on his own, could not afford childcare, was having financial issues, and needed to make repairs on the home. In a month or two, he felt they would possibly be in a better position to care for Brandon. The social worker expressed concern that these issues had not been discussed prior to Brandon's arrival in the home, especially the need for home repairs.

Brandon was returned to his previous foster home and the foster parent was provided with a referral for childcare. A Victim of Crime program referral was submitted by the social worker so that Brandon would be eligible to receive services if needed in the future.

A schedule for the parents' visits was established with the foster parents. All visits were to be supervised. Over the next two months, the mother's visits were inconsistent. The foster parents reported increasingly strained relations with the mother due to her being very critical of the foster parents, using profanity, and accusing the foster mother of lying. When confronted with the concerns communicated by the foster parents, the mother denied the events they described. A neutral visitation supervisor was assigned.

COURT PROCEEDINGS

Jurisdiction/Disposition Hearing

At the jurisdiction/disposition hearing, the agency recommended that the court find Brandon's father to be his presumed father for the purpose of the proceedings and order that both parents be provided with family reunification services.

The father's attorney objected to the substance abuse references in the court report and the requirement in his case plan that he test and enroll in a substance abuse class at the discretion of the social worker. The social worker testified that Brandon's father "presented incoherent and under the influence" at their first encounter. However, in the case notes documenting their initial interaction, the social worker had written: "father presents himself as a provider to the family … was very concerned about his child being in the system. … He is willing to cooperate fully with the agency. Dad remained calm during the long telephone conversation." Despite the conflicting evidence, the court declined to strike the testimony of the social worker and ordered the father to comply with his case plan, which included the testing requirement and allowed the social worker discretion to require him to participate in an outpatient drug program.

The mother's case plan required that she participate in individual therapy and anger management, complete a parenting education program, drug test, and enroll in outpatient substance abuse treatment. If she tested positive for drugs, or in any way failed to participate in the outpatient program, she was required to enter residential treatment. The mother had previous involvement with child welfare services and had failed to reunify with her older child, Brandon's half-brother. The prior case involved allegations of substance abuse and sexual abuse.

The mother's service objectives included: comply with all orders of the court; express anger appropriately and do not act negatively on impulses; stay sober and show ability to live free from alcohol dependency; drug test; do not break the law; and consistently and appropriately parent Brandon.

The father's service objectives focused on his being able to refrain from the use of drugs and establish sobriety; maintain a stable and suitable residence for himself and Brandon; and monitor Brandon's health, safety, and well-being. An additional service objective required that he demonstrate his ability to protect his son from substance abuse and any unsafe situations.

The father was required to participate in individual therapy, attend and complete a parent education program, and drug test at the discretion of the social worker. Upon evidence of drug use, he would be required to attend outpatient drug treatment.

After the hearing, the social worker met with the father and grandparents. The father was provided with a referral for drug testing. He requested referrals for therapy and parenting classes. He stated that he would wait to enroll in parenting class until Brandon's mother completed the program. The social worker completed a referral for the paternal grandfather to complete a background check as part of the relative placement screening process.

Two weeks later, Brandon's mother was released from jail. A team meeting was convened to discuss the case plans, Brandon's placement, provision of support for the parents, and visitation. Brandon's parents, maternal great-aunt, the dependency investigator, the placement social worker, Brandon's social worker, and a parent advocate participated. In addition to the case plan, they discussed the restraining order issued by the criminal court preventing the mother from having contact with Brandon and the steps to be taken to have the juvenile court rescind the order.

Despite the mother's inconsistency in maintaining contact with the social worker, the social worker received reports from service providers indicating that the mother was participating in programs required by her case plan. Regarding the mother's progress, case notes indicated the mother completed the required parent education program within 90 days of release from custody. She had been attending substance abuse treatment but had relapsed with THC. The provider recommended another 10 weeks and aftercare. The social worker sent a referral for individual counseling to the mother.

Three weeks after being released from custody, the mother contacted the child welfare agency, asking to be assigned a new social worker, explaining she had a conflict with her current social worker. She told the supervisor that the social worker was not supporting her or advocating for her regarding her positive drug tests for THC. The supervisor declined to assign a new social worker but referred the mother to the Parent Advocacy Program for additional support. (A parent advocate was not assigned for two months.)

The father, who had been testing biweekly, was reported to have had a positive test for THC, causing the social worker to be concerned about his unsupervised visits with Brandon. She contacted the caregiver who indicated that there was nothing in his behavior indicating he was under the influence of drugs or alcohol. Two weeks later, the social worker discovered that the positive test result was for another client, not the father. It is unclear from the case record whether the mistake was made by the social worker or the substance abuse testing service provider.

Six-Month Status Review Hearing

The status review court report summarized the progress of both parents on their case plans. The report described the mother as "in progress" on her case plan objectives. Two new objectives were added: The mother was to pay attention to and monitor Brandon's health, safety, and well-being and cooperate with the visitation plan which required she express anger appropriately and not act negatively on her impulses. Although the mother had several positive drug tests for marijuana early in the reporting period, her test results in recent months had been negative. Although the mother was reported as doing well in her outpatient substance abuse program, her counselor requested that the social worker amend the mother's case plan to require that she continue in the program for a full 28 weeks. The random drug testing requirement was reduced from three times per week to twice each week. The mother had also begun participating in weekly DUI classes as a condition of criminal probation.

Brandon's father was also described as being "in progress" on his objectives. New objectives were added: that he be willing and able to arrange appropriate childcare and supervision as needed and that he consistently, appropriately, and adequately parent his child.

The recommended plan was to reunify Brandon with his father; if reunification was unsuccessful, the agency would consider reunification with his mother. An adoption assessment was initiated due to Brandon's age.

After receiving notification that the father had completed his parenting classes, the social worker met with him to discuss going forward with reunification, as well as the father's relationship with the mother. Case notes indicate that the social worker advised him that if the parents intended to live together, doing so would "slow down reunification because the mother has more intensive services than he does but … being with the mother was not an automatic barrier to reunification." The social worker told the father that if they were planning to co-parent or reunify as a couple, they would have to enter couples counseling or similar joint counseling to improve their communication, because their conflicts were documented and a concern to the court. According to the case notes, Brandon's father stated that if being with the mother would slow down reunification with his son, he would choose to parent Brandon on his own.

One month after the status review hearing, the mother contacted the social worker and asked how much longer she needed to be in therapy. The social worker indicated she would need to get a report from her therapist. The therapist reported that Brandon's mother had terminated individual therapy against the therapist's recommendations. The mother continued to contact the social worker and express concerns. She consented to allow the social worker access to her records at the court-ordered DUI program; the report indicated she had attended 28 of a required 64 weeks of DUI classes during a nine-month period.

The family preservation worker who had been assigned to support reunification referred Brandon and his father for Parent-Infant Interactive Therapy services. The social worker informed the court that the agency would be initiating an extended trial home visit with the father and, if successful, the agency would recommend a change in the case plan to family maintenance with the father and termination of reunification services for the mother. It was recommended that the mother's reunification services be replaced with informal child welfare services. One month later, the social worker initiated the 30-day trial visit for Brandon at his father's home.

The visit began two weeks after the hearing and home visits were conducted by the social worker. Brandon seemed comfortable in his father's home and daycare had been arranged. Although the mother had been visiting, Brandon's father said he was having trouble with the mother because she had become hostile towards him as a result of the court orders which placed Brandon with him. The father admitted to the social worker that he was struggling with finances. They reviewed his budget to assess his needs and the social worker submitted a request for household supplies and furnishings.

Two months later, at an interim review hearing, the agency changed their recommendation to dismissal with sole physical custody to the father and reasonable visitation for the mother. Informal family maintenance services were extended to the father.

End of case record review.

DISCUSSION QUESTIONS

1. At the initial team meeting, it was decided that a reference in the case file to the father having a substance abuse history required the father to provide proof he was no longer using drugs. The team concluded it would be in Brandon's best interest to place him in an age-appropriate foster home and ask the father to begin drug testing.
    - What could have been done to maintain Brandon safely in his father's home?
    - How might Brandon and his father living with paternal grandparents have made a difference in maintaining him with his father?

2. Brandon had several placement moves in his first few weeks of care.
    - What do we know about how children can be affected when they experience multiple moves?

3. Brandon's grandfather contacted the social worker and stated that he and his wife were not able to care for Brandon. The summary does not provide any details about the conversation between the social worker and Brandon's grandfather.
    - What questions would you ask to make sure that you have an accurate understanding about what he meant by "the pressure was too much"?
    - What arrangements might have been made for the grandparents to address some of the concerns/barriers listed in the case summary?

4. The social worker expressed concern that the issues identified by the grandfather had not been discussed prior to Brandon's arrival in their home, especially the need for home repairs.
    - What should have been done prior to placement to identify the need for these home repairs?
    - What types of home repairs might create concerns for the social worker before placement?

5. Case notes at the end of the case record review indicate that the granting of custody to Brandon's father was creating tensions in the relationship between Brandon's parents.
    - What services would you recommend as part of the informal family maintenance support provided to Brandon's father to address these tensions?

Marilyn K.

Marilyn K. is a six-year-old girl whose mother had an extensive history with child welfare services, including failing to reunify with six older children, but was able to regain custody of Marilyn

FAMILY CONFIGURATION

Household Members

Marilyn: age 6
Mother: age 47

INITIAL RISKS AND HARMS

Child protection received a call from the school secretary at Marilyn's elementary school reporting that Marilyn's mother had not picked her up after school, adding that this was the twelfth time in three months she had failed to do so. When the mother arrived five hours later, according to the school secretary, she smelled of alcohol. The child welfare agency was called and the emergency response social worker interviewed the mother at the assessment center where Marilyn had been taken. Marilyn's mother acknowledged that she was homeless again and had not taken her psychotropic medications in some time. She denied any substance abuse issues, but admitted to "polishing off" the alcohol she had on her person before she arrived at the school. Case notes indicated that Marilyn's mother was verbally aggressive with the emergency response social worker. Agency records indicated that Marilyn's mother had extensive previous child welfare involvement with failed reunification cases for six previous children. Additional search in a state criminal index found that the mother was on parole for drug sales. The emergency response worker noted that Marilyn showed no signs of abuse or neglect.

FINDING A HOME FOR MARILYN

The assessment center social worker searched agency files for names and contact information for Marilyn's family. The mother said she wanted Marilyn placed with family. The worker was able to reach Marilyn's oldest sister (25) who agreed to be assessed for placement. In the interim, Marilyn was placed in a licensed foster home until her adult sister could be assessed. Other maternal relatives contacted by the social worker expressed concerns about this adult sister as a caregiver for Marilyn, but indicated that they were unable to care for her. Marilyn's mother also reported concern about several maternal relatives as placement options, specifically her father and her former stepmother. Ultimately Marilyn was placed with a non-related extended family member who had known Marilyn all her life and was a licensed county foster care provider. Marilyn's mother agreed with the placement.

COURT PROCEEDINGS

Jurisdiction/Disposition Hearing

The mother had a substantial history with child welfare services that included seven older children being made dependents of the court. Six of these children did not reunify with the mother, including an infant who had been adopted four years previously following termination of parental rights. As a result, the social worker recommended that the court bypass the mother for reunification services and set a hearing to terminate her parental rights. The social worker's assessment of the mother stated that she had never fully addressed or taken responsibility for her substance abuse, blamed her situation on external circumstances, and struggled with homelessness, which resulted in the removal of seven other children from her custody.

Marilyn's mother contested the recommendation to bypass reunification services, citing her enrollment in a comprehensive residential drug treatment program as an exception to the statutory provision for bypass. The mother's attorney also argued that despite his client's periodic homelessness and mental stability challenges, Marilyn did not show signs of abuse or neglect and was very bonded to her mother. The attorney set a contested hearing and successfully argued that his client should be offered services to reunify with Marilyn. After hearing the testimony of the social worker and the mother, the court agreed that the mother demonstrated commitment to her sobriety and to maintaining a safe and stable home for herself and Marilyn

The mother's case plan objectives corresponded to her long-term issues with substance use and housing instability. She was required to demonstrate that she could express anger appropriately and not act negatively on impulses, stay sober and show ability to live free from alcohol dependency and drugs, test clean as required, obtain and maintain a stable and suitable residence for herself and Marilyn, and obtain and keep a job.

Her case plan required compliance with the conditions of the residential treatment program, adding random drug testing and a psychological evaluation. She was ordered to complete one year of outpatient substance abuse services following the residential program and to obtain employment and housing. The case plan concurrent goal was adoption.

Six-Month Status Review Hearing

The court report categorized the mother's progress on her case plan as "substantial." In the six months between Marilyn's removal from her mother and the six-month review hearing, Marilyn's mother lived in the residential treatment program. She continued to make progress on her case plan, including participating in individual counseling, and regularly tested negative for substances.

At the six-month status review, the court ordered continued reunification services. Marilyn's mother had completed her inpatient program on time and had moved into transitional housing. In the social worker's conversations with the mother's relatives, there was general agreement that she appeared to be "more engaged and motivated than they had ever seen her."

The report indicated that the mother consistently urged the social worker to authorize more visits with her daughter. Two months after the disposition hearing, the caregiver notified the social worker that Marilyn's mother had been bringing her intimate partner to the weekly supervised visit without permission of the social worker. The social worker counseled the mother about her responsibilities and she provided information about her partner. Therapeutic visits were initiated for Marilyn and her mother. The original court order that all visits be supervised was changed after the third month; visits were increased to include weekends at the program, and after four months, Marilyn had weekly overnight supervised visits with her mother at the program. One month later, the clinician providing therapeutic visitation recommended that the requirement be removed, and described the mother and Marilyn as having a secure and healthy bond.

Twelve-Month Status Review Hearing

In the 12-month permanency report, the social worker again described the mother's progress as "substantial." The court report indicated that Marilyn's mother had worked on her case plan without incident. She had completed her inpatient program and graduated from her parenting class. Her case plan was revised to require that the mother participate in a 12-step or equivalent program.

Marilyn's mother had been placed in transitional housing as an extension of her residential treatment program. Marilyn had been placed with her mother on an extended visit prior to the hearing. The social worker recommended to the court that Marilyn be returned to her mother's care with family maintenance services. The agency agreed to provide a transportation pass for Marilyn's mother so that Marilyn could remain at her current school. The court ordered an additional six months of reunification services.

Eighteen-Month Status Review Hearing

Marilyn consistently did well in her mother's care and her mother maintained her sobriety in the months between status review hearings. Due to the mother's progress, the case plan for Marilyn was changed from return home to remain home. The mother's case plan objectives and requirements were amended to focus on her parenting responsibilities regarding Marilyn's school and overall well-being. Drug testing was reduced to biweekly.

An incident of domestic violence came to the social worker's attention shortly before the hearing. Transitional housing program staff reported a domestic incident between Marilyn's mother and her boyfriend at the program; Marilyn was visiting with an aunt for the weekend. The social worker ordered that Marilyn remain with the aunt until the mother could be interviewed.

Shortly thereafter, Marilyn and her mother were evicted from the transitional housing program due to the mother asking another resident to watch Marilyn, which was in violation of the house rules. The mother notified the social worker on the following day, stating that she was staying with friends and family and was on the waiting list for a local family shelter.

After a team meeting and further assessment of Marilyn, consensus was reached that Marilyn's mother had made significant progress and was very bonded to her daughter and parenting well. Since she had found housing in a family shelter, continued family maintenance services would be recommended to the court. Marilyn continued to do well in school, reported she liked her school and teachers, and was involved in school activities. Two weeks after Marilyn and her mother moved into the shelter, the mother's boyfriend appeared at the shelter intoxicated, and he and the mother engaged in a verbal argument. Shelter staff intervened and removed the boyfriend. Marilyn was spending the night with an aunt and did not witness the event. Marilyn's mother explained to the social worker that she would not have spoken with the boyfriend if Marilyn was with her.

The family maintenance social worker maintained close contact with the mother, helping her identify resources and supports to decrease the likelihood of relapse. Housing and income continued to be the mother's most urgent needs. Shortly before the status review, the maternal grandmother unexpectedly passed away. The mother was able to maintain her sobriety and remain in contact with her social worker. She discussed with her social worker how the death of her mother affected her and what she did to maintain her sobriety.

At the end of the case record review, Marilyn's mother continued to struggle with housing. Since they had exceeded the six-month time limit at the shelter, the social worker assisted the mother in applying for subsidized housing. She was accepted into the program, but had been unable to locate a suitable residence. As a result, Marilyn and her mother moved into her grandmother's home with the mother's adult son. The agency requested continued family maintenance services at the status review hearing due to ongoing concerns about the mother's ability to obtain and maintain stable housing and find employment.

End of case record review.

DISCUSSION QUESTIONS

1. In conducting assessments, it is important to be aware of your own beliefs, values, perceptions, and other underlying circumstances that may have the potential to cause bias and may cause you to filter out information needed to make accurate assessments.

   - Identify your own negative reactions or biases toward this family.
   - How might you overcome these biases or assumptions?

2. What service providers would you need outside of foster care or the child welfare agency to assist in creating a plan for this family?

   - What questions might you ask the parent to identify family supports?
   - What might you ask the child?

3. What are your thoughts about social workers giving more weight to allegations or other information from professionals than to those coming from members of the public or family?

4. When Marilyn and her mother lost their housing, what might have been absent from the information collected that would have changed the social worker's mind about removing Marilyn from her mother's care?

   - How might the social worker have engaged in safety planning related to those concerns?

5. Thinking of the investigation only, imagine that a social worker has gathered and organized all the initial information. This case is transferred to you and you recognize some potential bias on the part of the previous social worker which you believe affected the outcome of the referral.

   - What do you do to acknowledge this and how would you address this situation?

Ronald R.

Ronald R. is a 10-year-old boy adopted out of foster care, raised with another adoptive boy who became increasingly out of control as they reached pre-teen years

FAMILY CONFIGURATION

Household Members

Ronald: age 10, adopted by the mother at age 4 through a child welfare agency
Mother: adoptive parent of Ronald and his adoptive brother, age not specified in case record
Older brother: age 11, also adopted from foster care by Ronald's mother

INITIAL RISKS AND HARMS

This case began with an allegation of general neglect with respect to Ronald's mother. The referral alleged that the older brother was extremely aggressive, impulsive, and had physically assaulted Ronald and his mother. Ronald's mother told the emergency response social worker that the boys were out of control and she was overwhelmed. She said that in recent years both boys had become increasingly violent, angry, and disruptive. The boys used profanity, called her names, and had defaced the home by writing the word "bitch" on several places on the living room and kitchen walls. She said that their behavior had caused the family to lose their housing on several occasions because apartment management refused to renew their lease. She said that she had lost her childcare business and her home because of the boys' behavior and defiance, and that in some months she barely made enough money to care for the family. The mother acknowledged that police were constantly in and out of her home because of the boys' behavior and both boys had been hospitalized on 48-hour involuntary psychiatric holds. Reluctantly, she admitted she had considered having one of her sons removed; however, she said she would feel like "a failure" as a mother if she did so.

Ronald had been adopted when he was four years old and his brother, who was not biologically related, had been adopted the following year. According to their mother, she had adopted them as toddlers through a child welfare agency. Both boys had experienced extensive trauma in their birth families according to the information provided to her by the child welfare agency. Ronald had been diagnosed with oppositional defiant disorder (ODD) and was being reassessed for an Individualized Education Plan (IEP).

Ronald's mother reported that the county where she adopted the boys had been very responsive to her needs for support since the adoption and had provided an array of services including Wraparound services and in-home therapy. Each morning, Wraparound staff came to her home to help get the boys to school. Due to these ongoing services, the initial team assessment advised that additional services and support not be offered. After some reconsideration, the agency elected to offer Ronald's mother informal family maintenance (IFM) services. In the 12 months prior to the current referral, there had been 5 referrals for general neglect and 2 for physical abuse, all of which had been either evaluated out or were unfounded. A team meeting was held and the mother agreed to IFM services. Service objectives for the mother included arranging for appropriate childcare and supervision in her absence; showing her ability to supervise her children in all settings; and monitoring her children's health, safety, and well-being, including providing for their special needs and consistently and appropriately parenting. She also agreed to individual therapy, to participate in a medication evaluation and take medication if prescribed, and to attend a parenting education program.

Approximately two months later, Ronald was brought to the county assessment center following an incident during which he hit his mother. The police had been called after Ronald refused to go to school and began throwing rocks and using his fists on his mother. Ronald's mother confirmed that she could not care for him and felt unsafe. After being removed, Ronald was described in case notes as being "distraught" and repeatedly asking to go home.

FINDING A HOME FOR RONALD

After a team meeting which included Ronald's mother, it was decided that placement in a Foster Family Agency (FFA) home would best address Ronald's needs. Ronald's mother told the social worker that she was not ready to take Ronald home. Ronald did not want to live in a home with a foster father. The home identified for the placement had a single foster mother who already had another foster child from a neighboring county in her home.

Despite wanting to be returned to his mother and his school, Ronald was reported to be doing well at the foster home, including making major improvements in his behavior. Service providers discussed his progress with Ronald's social worker and were in agreement that Ronald appeared to be intelligent, kind, and capable of controlling himself when not in his mother's care or around his older brother. Ronald repeatedly asked his social worker to send him home and asked to be allowed to return to his school.

Mason T.

21

Mason T. is a teenage boy whose family received family maintenance services for two years until Mason was arrested, declared a ward of the juvenile court, and placed out of home

FAMILY CONFIGURATION

Household Members

Mason: age 15
Mother: age 52
Father: age 49

INITIAL RISKS AND HARMS

This began as a family maintenance case which involved a family of three, including mother, father, and son Mason. Mason was then removed from his mother's care and placed in the juvenile detention center 17 months after case initiation. Mason was under the jurisdiction of the child welfare agency and was a ward of the court due to juvenile offenses.

During the case Mason experienced nine placements, beginning with his initial placement at home. Mason's older sister who was also under the age of 18 was in the care of their maternal grandmother. There was a brief mention of a maternal grandfather, but based upon the case record he did not appear to be involved with the family. There was also an older brother noted to be living in the home for a short period of time but he similarly was not otherwise mentioned in the case record. There had been several previous child protective service reports made regarding verbal and physical abuse in the home, but none of these reports were substantiated. Mason had a history of being placed on involuntary psychiatric holds when he was found to be a danger to himself or a danger to others because of his violent outbursts.

The police had been called to the home on numerous occasions related to a history of violent altercations between Mason and his father. The event that brought the family to the attention of the child welfare agency involved the father being arrested for stabbing Mason with a fishing knife during an altercation that caused approximately 11 superficial wounds. It was reported that when the mother attempted to intervene, she was stabbed in the palm of her hand. The father was intoxicated at the time of the stabbing incident, and the mother admitted that the father was aggressive and abusive towards Mason. The mother stated however that the altercation was Mason's fault and that she wanted her husband released back home. Mason stayed in the home with the mother because the father was incarcerated. Family maintenance services were ordered for the mother and father, although a restraining order was issued between Mason and the father. Throughout the case there were concerns that the mother and father were not following the stay away order.

There were financial and resource related concerns throughout the case. The mother's car was removed as evidence in the criminal matter at case start and was never returned to her, which created problems related to transportation and service engagement. The mother and father filed for bankruptcy at the start of the case. Shortly after the case began, Mason and his mother were evicted from their home and lived in hotel rooms and camped in tents.

Mason was placed on four involuntary psychiatric holds during the 24 months of the case record. The first hold occurred because he choked his mother. The second hold occurred because he held a knife to his throat and threatened to kill himself. The third occurred because Mason head butted a staff member at his school. The final hold occurred when he became upset because he could not find his bong (drug paraphernalia), and he ended up on the roof of a building threatening to hurt himself.

FINDING A HOME FOR MASON

Mason remained in the care of his mother for the first 17 months of the case. While in the care of his mother, the father remained out of the home because of a stay away order issued by the court. During these 17 months the mother and Mason moved from their family home to an apartment and then were evicted from the apartment. Following the eviction, the mother and Mason were homeless. They stayed in motels as well as campgrounds. They could not live with the maternal grandmother because the father was living with her, and they were unable to live in shelters because of their dog.

At about 17 months, the older sister came into the home and threatened Mason with a hammer and bat. The sister was arrested and placed on house arrest with the maternal grandmother. Mason was then placed in juvenile hall for about two and a half months. After being released from juvenile hall, Mason went to the assessment center for one day, and then he was taken to his first group home. During his first day in the group home, a drive-by shooting occurred on the street. Mason ran away from the group home and the mother found him a place to stay for the night. The next day Mason returned to the assessment center for two days.

Mason then went to his second group home. Mason had lived in this group home for about one week when they gave a seven-day notice because he was not participating in the program; however, the seven-day notice was rescinded several days later. A few days after the group home rescinded their seven-day notice Mason removed his ankle monitor. Mason then returned to juvenile hall for five days. After another brief stay at the assessment center, Mason was taken by child protective services to his third group home, which was located out of county. Mason remained in this placement for the remainder of the case review.

COURT PROCEEDINGS
Six-Month Status Review Hearing

The child welfare agency recommended that Mason stay in the home and the mother and father continue to receive family maintenance services. The judge was concerned with the lack of progress, and therapeutic behavioral services were ordered, along with supervised therapeutic visitation between the father and Mason. Another social worker was assigned to the case, and the mother stated it was not fair that they kept changing workers on her family.

The initial case plan included Mason, his mother, and father. The service objectives for Mason focused on staying sober, attending school, and not acting aggressively. These objectives remained relatively constant throughout the case record. Mason was expected to attend school, counseling, and drug testing. Mason did not follow through with his service objectives for most of the case record review. Mason did not attend school regularly where he was supposed to receive many of the services detailed in the case plan. Once placed out of his mother's home, Mason did begin treatment services, engaged in drug testing, and regularly attended school.

The service objectives for the mother were focused on keeping Mason safe, away from the abuser (his father), not being a victim of further domestic violence, complying with psychological evaluation and treatment, and accepting responsibility for her actions. The mother was expected to attend weekly counseling, parent education classes, substance abuse treatment, and drug testing. The mother complied with the parenting education classes and initially followed through with the counseling. The mother did not participate in substance abuse treatment and did not regularly drug test. The mother contended throughout the case that she believed she did not need these services, and she completed a hair follicle drug test that was negative. The mother did not keep Mason and father away from each other when Mason was in her care.

The service objectives for the father required him to stay sober, not contact Mason, follow through with his probation, take responsibility for his actions, and express his anger appropriately. The father was expected to attend domestic violence classes and engage in substance abuse treatment, drug testing, psychological care (medication), and counseling. There was a stay away order between Mason and the father for the entirety of the case, but the father and Mason did participate in a few family counseling sessions. About 18 months into the case the father was removed from the case plan. There is no mention in the case record as to why this occurred.

Twelve-Month Status Review Hearing

The child welfare agency recommended that Mason remain in the care of the mother that and the mother and father receive six more months of family maintenance services. The therapeutic behavioral therapist worker and family therapist wanted Mason removed from the mother's care based on a lack of progress and Mason's behavior. The judge set a 30-day interim review hearing. If Mason was not attending school at that point, placement in a residential setting would be considered. The family therapist refused to work with the family until Mason was in school and the family had stable housing.

Interim Review Hearing

The child welfare agency recommended that Mason remain in the custody of his mother and the family receive six more months of family maintenance services. Mason had attended three out of seven days of school during the month. The case was continued for six months.

Eighteen-Month Status Review Hearing

At the 18-month status review, it was reported that Mason was detained in juvenile hall. There were no county foster homes or Foster Family Agencies (FFAs) who would take Mason given his behaviors and mental status. Approval was granted to seek a higher level of care in a group home. Mason had a GPS tracking anklet until he was in his placement. Mason ran away from the group home his first day after a drive-by shooting occurred outside. Mason was scared and called his mother, who, against advice, picked up Mason and found him a place to stay for the evening.

Mason was taken to the assessment center by child welfare and was accepted into a group home located out of county. His mother refused to sign the case plan and said her son was now the problem of the child welfare agency. The agency offered the mother mileage reimbursement and/or train tickets to visit Mason. The agency approved a day-long visit between Mason and his mother but, because she was not participating in her drug treatment program, would not allow an overnight visit.

The father had not participated in his case plan since the previous hearing.

The child welfare agency held a meeting to assess Mason's "emotionally disturbed" status (no determination was noted in the case record following the meeting).

It was decided that Mason would be discharged from probation on the condition that he do well in school, at the group home, and in substance abuse and anger management counseling.

About 18 months into the case the father was removed from the case plan. There is no mention in the case record as to why this occurred, and reunification services to the father were terminated without court order.

End of case record review.

DISCUSSION QUESTIONS

1. The mother was refused an overnight visit because she did not participate in a drug program.
    - What conflicting information did you identify in the case summary that might lead you as a new social worker to explore this decision?
    - What might you do differently?
2. Structured Decision Making (SDM) is an evidence- and research-based system that assists in identifying the key points in the progress of a child welfare case and uses structured assessments to improve the consistency and validity of decisions.
    - How would a tool like this be important when determining which evidenced-based services should be offered and assessing reunification readiness?
    - What concerns do you have about utilizing a tool like this?
3. Thinking about the difference in objectives/philosophy between the child welfare services and juvenile probation systems, what difficulties do you anticipate when working with this youth?
    - Do you see any commonalities?
4. Mason spends much of his time in a group home.
    - What are the expectations of placement in group homes versus placement with families or foster homes?
    - What concerns do you have with group home placements?
5. Mason is a teenager.
    - What independent living skills services might you add to Mason's case plan to help him with becoming a non-minor dependent?
    - If Mason chooses to leave foster care at 18, would your plan for independent living skills change for Mason?
    - Explain your thinking.

6. What is Mason's father's role in the case?
    *   How might you have worked with him?
    *   What do you think happened to Mason's father to cause him to withdraw from the case?
    *   What might you have done to encourage his engagement?
7. What might you have done to help Mason's mother find stability and engage in services?
8. Mason's mother said there were too many social workers.
    *   How do you think this affected or could affect the outcome of the case?

Noah M.

Noah M. is a seven-year-old boy removed from his parents due to their methamphetamine use, mother's refusal to admit her substance abuse, father's delusional tendencies, and a history of domestic violence

FAMILY CONFIGURATION

Household Members

Noah: age 7
Older sister: age 12, half-sibling
Mother: age not specified in case record
Father: age not specified in case record

INITIAL RISKS AND HARMS

Noah's mother called 911 saying she was afraid of her husband and needed help protecting their seven-year-old son. She explained that the previous night she had found Noah's father standing over him with a can of cooking spray, spraying him, and chanting biblical verses. She told the police she had calmed her husband down and they all went to bed. The morning following this incident, she found the father locked in their car with Noah. She was able to get Noah out of the car and locked him into the bathroom with her, where she called the police on her cellphone.

The police came to the home and arrested Noah's father for intoxication and called child welfare services. The emergency response social worker took Noah and his older half-sister into custody due to the father's intoxication and history of dangerous and abusive behavior, and the mother's inability to protect the children from his behaviors.

The child welfare services investigation revealed that police had been called to the home on numerous occasions regarding domestic violence. The father had been detained on a 48-hour psychiatric hold the previous week. The police offered an emergency protective order, but the mother did not follow up. Police reports indicated that the father was taking methamphetamines, experiencing delusions, and was frequently out of control.

Child welfare agency records contained 15 prior referrals for general neglect, each involving Noah's half-sister alone. All the referrals were determined to be unfounded, evaluated out, or inconclusive. Six referrals had occurred in the prior year.

FINDING A HOME FOR NOAH

Noah was detained for one day in emergency shelter and returned to his mother the following day after being evaluated for medical needs. Noah's half-sister was released to the care of her biological father, with whom she lived most of the time, spending every other weekend during the school year and every other week during the summer with her mother.

When the mother was interviewed the day after the event triggering Noah's removal, the emergency response worker discussed how Noah could be protected in her home and what was required of her to retain custody of him. An action plan was written including a personal safety plan. The investigator also explained the consequences of Noah being removed from her by the court. Two weeks later, the social worker obtained an emergency placement referral from the court and removed Noah from his mother and took him to the children's' shelter again. The removal was based on additional risk factors that had been identified, including methamphetamine use by the mother and the mother's failure to comply with the restraining order issued against the father. In addition, the father had reported that the mother had told him "she had done something bad and was going to give up Noah" and commit suicide. The mother denied the conversation.

The social worker immediately contacted Noah's paternal grandparents who said they were willing to have Noah placed in their home, which required an expedited health and safety plan including a corrective action plan related to gun safety.

The child protection investigation following Noah's removal substantiated allegations of caretaker absence/incapacity as to Noah's father. In addition, the father had been convicted of domestic violence and the court had issued a restraining order prohibiting him from any contact with his family. The father indicated to the social worker that he wanted to discuss how he could reconnect with his family and stated he was worried Noah was being sexually abused by their housemate.

The investigation also confirmed the mother's substance use when the social worker received a report that the mother's hair follicle drug test came back positive for "constant use of methamphetamines" and her urine test came back positive for current use of methamphetamines. The mother continued to deny using drugs. Case notes show the mother leaving messages for the social worker denying she was an addict and asserting she "should not have to complete drug treatment … and is not financially stable enough to complete any program." Noah's mother reported to the social worker that she had obtained a temporary restraining order and she had been fired from her job working for her father-in-law. Noah's father violated the restraining order by entering their home to retrieve his toiletries. Police put out a warrant for his arrest.

Visitation was arranged for both parents with Noah. At a supervised visit between Noah and his mother at the social worker's office, the paternal grandmother told the social worker they were worried that the father had been inside the grandparents' home while they were away because they received voicemails from him from their home telephone number. The grandmother also told the social worker that Noah's father was at her house yesterday to shower and "it was difficult to keep him out of the home because he is homeless right now."

After Noah was placed with his grandparents, a team meeting was convened to prepare a service plan. Although there was no evidence that Noah had been a victim of the domestic violence between his parents and he had not been the subject of prior referrals, concerns were expressed about possible effects of his exposure to the interactions between his parents and his half-sister. It was agreed that Noah would benefit from individual therapeutic services, and the parents would be expected to participate in collateral sessions as requested by the therapist. After a few sessions, Noah's clinician reported concerns about Noah's sexualized behaviors, poor boundaries, and aggressive play. The team discussed the likelihood that these were signs of trauma and recommended that Noah be interviewed by specialized sex abuse staff. The result of the interview was inconclusive for sex abuse.

Seven months into his placement with his grandparents, the social worker began to receive messages from the grandparents regarding problems with Noah. The social worker met them at their home. The grandparents were very upset with his behavior, reporting they could maintain the placement for a while longer, but his behavior was getting worse and hard to handle. The social worker met with Noah's therapist to discuss his behavior and the grandparents' parenting. As a result of the meeting, it was decided family therapy should begin.

During this period both the mother and father had been working on their case plans and generally making progress toward their goals. Visitation between the parents and Noah had been gradually transitioned from supervised, to limited periods unsupervised, to full days, to overnights and after six months, to weekends with his mother. Case notes and reports from his therapist indicate that Noah was responding well to the increased contact with his parents and had not expressed any apprehension. Noah reported he enjoyed weekend visits with his mother and wanted to spend more time with his father.

After a team meeting including grandparents, providers, and therapist, it was decided that Noah would be returned to the care of his mother if the father moved out of the home and they participated in services to support their relationships, such as family therapy and couples therapy. The parents agreed.

Approximately a month after Noah was returned to his mother, the parents were separated and eventually couples therapy and family therapy were terminated due to the father missing too many appointments. The father was also dismissed from his outpatient drug treatment program and domestic violence classes because of missing too many appointments.

COURT PROCEEDINGS

Jurisdiction/Disposition Hearing

The child protection agency filed a petition requesting that Noah be declared a dependent child and removed from the care, custody, and control of his parents based on evidence of caretaker absence/incapacity, and the parents be offered family reunification services. The main concerns arising from the social worker's assessment of the mother's protective capacity were her substance use and denial of use, violation of the restraining order against the father, and inability to deal with stressors. In addition, the mother had 15 previous child protection referrals for Noah's sister. There were serious concerns based on this history of Noah's mother's ability to protect the children from the father's erratic and abusive behavior. The report described the father's abuse of methamphetamines, delusional and violent behavior, and the parents' persistent pattern of domestic violence.

The mother's service objectives were the following: show your ability and willingness to have custody of your child; comply with all orders of the court; stay free from illegal drugs and show your ability to live free from drug dependency; drug test as required; protect your child from emotional harm; monitor your child's health, safety, and well-being; do not behave in a manner that is verbally, emotionally, physically, or sexually abusive or threatening; and show you can accept responsibility for your actions.

The mother's case plan required that she 1) participate in a program of individual therapy, in part to specifically address the discord and violence issues within the parental relationship and develop more appropriate ways to address conflict and 2) complete a substance abuse treatment program including drug testing, with the level of treatment to be determined by the treatment program staff in consultation with the social worker.

The father's services objectives were the following: comply with medical or psychological treatment; comply with all orders of the court; stay free from illegal drugs and show your ability to live free from drug dependency; comply with all required drug tests; show ability and willingness to have custody of your child; monitor your child's health, safety, and well-being; do not behave in a manner that is verbally, emotionally, physically, or sexually abusive or threatening; protect your child from emotional harm; and show you can accept responsibility for your actions.

The father's case plan also required him to participate in a program of individual therapy, in part to specifically address the discord and violence issues within the parental relationship and develop more appropriate ways to address conflict. He was also required to complete a substance abuse treatment program including drug testing, level of treatment to be determined by the program staff in consultation with the social worker. In addition, Noah's father was required to cooperate with a psychological and psychotropic medications evaluation and follow any treatment recommendations made as a result of the evaluations.

The social worker's notes reflected receiving multiple voicemails from the father after the hearing, venting about his economic situation, his relationship with Noah's mother, and the child welfare agency's involvement in their lives. The father's speech was described in the notes as "slurred" and very slow. Two days later, the father contacted the social worker again, reporting that he was trying to find work and had been too busy to enroll in a substance abuse program, but he assured the social worker that he would make an appointment. The father also apologized for his voicemails stating that he had been drinking, should not have called, and would like to get back on track and focus on his case plan.

In an office meeting, case notes document that the social worker gave the mother some materials to help her with her case plan, including a successful reunification tips brochure, an agency flow chart, parent orientation information, and contact information for substance abuse treatment and mental health service providers. In addition, the social worker explained the agency parent support program, stressed how valuable the program had been to other parents, and re-referred the mother to the parent advocate program. The mother told the social worker she had called the police the previous night and filed a police report, because the father had come to her house. The father was arrested.

In a meeting with the father, the social worker gave him similar materials and explained that, until the juvenile court had reviewed the current stay away order and determined visiting with his father was in Noah's best interest, visits would be postponed. The social worker indicated a special hearing had been scheduled and she would recommend supervised visitation with Noah.

The social worker was subsequently notified Noah's father had been arrested and was incarcerated. The social worker interviewed him in jail. According to the case notes, the father told the social worker he was interested in residential substance abuse treatment if it meant he would be released from jail. Two weeks later, Noah's father was released to a residential treatment program.

In discussions with Noah, he told the social worker he was ready to visit his father. The social worker obtained approval for a supervised visit at the treatment program.

Case notes reflected the mother was making progress in her substance abuse program and had consistently given clean tests in the past two months. However, one month later, the mother's parent advocate notified the social worker she was closing the case because the mother had not returned her phone calls.

Six-Month Status Review Hearing

The status review report described the parents' progress on their service objectives as "in progress." The social worker recommended all existing orders remain in effect, Noah remain in out-of-home placement, and the parents continue receiving family reunification services. The report identified primary concerns for each parent (i.e., the mother continued to minimize her substance abuse; the father had been minimally complying with his case plan and minimized his substance abuse, blaming the mother for introduction of drugs into the home).

At the request of the juvenile court, the criminal court amended its stay away order to allow supervised contact with Noah, written communication between parents, and supervised contact between the parents.

Three months after the status review hearing, the mother was referred to a specialized support social worker to assist with reunification.

After completing six months of residential treatment, the father notified the social worker he had checked himself out of residential treatment because the criminal court ordered he complete a minimum of six months of treatment (even though the program lasted one year).

The father petitioned the criminal court to amend the stay away order, with the expectation the father would be moving back in with his family. The father was successful; the order was amended and the social worker began to discuss a slow transition home with the parents.

At the end of the review period, the social worker's case notes indicated the father had completed five of 52 domestic violence classes required by the criminal court, had completed his psychiatric evaluation, and had attended five individual therapy sessions. Visits with Noah are described in the case notes as "going well."

Twelve-Month Status Review Hearing

At the 12-month hearing, the social worker recommended Noah remain a dependent and remain in out-of-home placement and recommended that the parents receive an additional six months of reunification services. The mother had been complying with the case plan, attending every visitation with Noah and visits had gone well. The same information was provided about Noah's father's progress.

The social worker also recommended an interim review hearing be set for consideration of returning Noah to his mother in the next 60 days. One month after the hearing, Noah and his mother began Thursday and Sunday visits and the father moved out of the home. The social worker required father and mother begin couples counseling to focus on violence within the parental relationship. Opportunities for the father to have unsupervised visits with Noah were linked to his progress in these sessions.

At the interim review hearing, the social worker reported the mother was not ready to have Noah in her care without support and recommended family maintenance services. The social worker described complicated family dynamics, the pressure felt by the mother from her work and services schedule, and the possibility her home would be foreclosed. In addition, the mother disclosed she and the father had been arguing about marital separation and did not want to be required to meet with the father outside of structured settings because "it was too hard for her." The social worker met with each parent individually to discuss the importance of family/couples counseling and what marital separation could mean regarding the custody of Noah. One month later, couples counseling was terminated because father was inconsistent in attending; the mother continued with individual counseling.

After hearing from their family counselor, the social worker met with the father to discuss his case plan. He explained he was having trouble with his job and transportation and wanted to work on his sobriety. He explained he had trouble getting reinstated into his drug treatment program but had an appointment the following day. The social worker contacted the father's counselor the following day who reported the father had missed his reinstatement appointment and too many domestic violence classes and was likely to be discharged. When the social worker contacted father, he admitted he had problems with the classes due to his work schedule and he would not be able to continue with family therapy because of his work schedule. The social worker discussed a father parenting support group with Noah's father which met in the evenings and referred him to the program.

The mother's counselor at her substance abuse treatment program reported to the social worker that her prognosis was good and they would be working on a transition plan, including continued support, random testing, and individual counseling. The mother informed the social worker she had a job and was confident she could parent Noah without agency support. Noah had been diagnosed with PTSD and inappropriate sexualized behavior and the social worker authorized continuing individual therapy. He continued to do well at school after being returned to his mother, with above average grades.

Approximately 18 months after the initial investigation, the family reunification services for the father were terminated. Supervised visitation (one time/week for two hours) continued between Noah and his father at his treatment program. Two years after Noah was removed from his home, dependency was dismissed and individual and family therapy were continued through informal family maintenance services to the mother.

End of case record review.

DISCUSSION QUESTIONS

1. Describe the importance of the mother's willingness to get a restraining order or protective order against the father.

2. What is the significance of father's employment conflicting with treatment and/or case plan tasks?
   - How would you help make arrangements around his work schedule?

3. How do you foresee the parent advocate working with the parent?
   - Do you think this happened?
   - Where do you think this failed?

4. There is mention of Noah having sexualized behavior.
   - Did you see any signs of why this type of behavior might be occurring?
   - What questions might you ask yourself or the parents to be able to identify if this behavior was age appropriate or due to trauma?

5. What concerns do you have, if any, with the father living in the grandparents' home?
   - How would you ameliorate these concerns?

6. What are your thoughts about child protection requiring the father to leave the home?
   - Please explain your concerns about separating Noah and his father and your concerns about their remaining in the same home.

APPENDIX A
Instructor Materials

FACILITATING CASE-BASED LEARNING

Teaching cases are used to create a learner-centered educational environment for self-directed inquiry about different interventions related to multi-problem situations, models of practice, and/or new ways of conceptualizing practice (Cossom, 1991; Jones, 2003). Case-based teaching and learning provides a problem-solving laboratory to identify multiple alternatives to diverse situations (Kimball, 1995). Through discussion and dialogue, students learn new ways of looking at situations that challenge attitudes and mindsets while learning to make decisions based on the available information (Webster, 1988). Cossom (1991) identifies several skills that case-based teaching can promote: 1) learning how to make judgments based on facts and articulated values rather than only assumptions, 2) applying and adapting conceptual and theoretical knowledge to complex and chaotic real-life situations, 3) making decisions in the context of competing alternatives, 4) learning to deal with differences of opinion among colleagues, 5) making use of colleagues as potential resources, and 6) presenting one's ideas and analysis that calls on the skills of verbal communication, influence, and debate. Learning through case-based teaching not only helps learners apply the knowledge required but does so within a context that they may encounter in the future.

Some of the benefits of case-based learning include 1) simulate practice dilemmas in order to test the understanding of participants as well as refine their skills in situations that simulate actual practice, 2) "level the learning field" by giving learners the same opportunity to contribute to a case discussion irrespective of their prior experience, 3) provide a safe learning environment to take risks as well as opportunities to frame probing questions and weighing alternatives before acting (this process is not always possible to learn in agency internships but clearly available in case-based learning), 4) help learners identify and articulate their own mental models related to their operating assumptions and alternative approaches to decision-making, and 5) provide an opportunity for case-based learning to complement field-based learning. Social work education programs that utilize case-based learning often seek to combine the features of complexity found in business school cases with the problem-based learning approach of medical school cases (Altshuler & Bosch, 2003; Ferguson, 2005).

Adapted from M. J. Austin and T. Packard, "Case-based Learning: Educating Future Human Service Managers," *Journal of Teaching in Social Work*, vol. 29, no. 2, pp. 216-236. Copyright © 2009 by Taylor & Francis Group.

CASE-BASED TEACHING

Case-based teaching requires a different approach to the teaching and learning process, especially modified classroom environments that support small group discussions (Cossom, 1991). Since there is no single correct teaching method for utilizing cases, instructors need to find an approach that builds upon their philosophy of teaching and assists them in reaching their course objectives. The following elements of case-based teaching are helpful to take into account: preparing learners, preparing instructors, selecting cases, and case reflection strategies.

Preparing Learners

Irrespective of one's orientation to learning, the process of case-based teaching needs to be explained and can use the following guidelines developed by Wassermann (1994) and Lynn (1999):

1. Describe how case-based learning differs from lecture-based teaching, the overall goals of cases, and the different expectations for the learners and instructor.

2. Explain the benefits of the case method and how they address the overall learning goals.

3. Communicate an understanding of the challenges that case-based learning might present, especially for those accustomed to a very different approach.

4. Explain the shift from searching for "answers" often associated with the lecture mode of instruction to the experiential approach of "examination" associated with case analysis and discussion, especially transitioning from the passive mode of learning associated with lectures to more interactive case-based learning.

5. Provide learners with information about evaluation procedures, especially for those who are concerned about what they need to do to succeed in mastering the learning experiences and identify lessons learned.

6. Since some learners require considerable time to make the transition to case-based learning, they might need multiple reminders about its purpose along with instructor patience in dealing with potential resistance.

7. When introducing the first few cases, it is helpful to assist students with case preparation (e.g., how to read a case and the discussion questions, how to anticipate an array of responses in class discussion, and how to read with a more critical eye).

Preparing Instructors

The use of case-based teaching is not only a shift for learners, but also a substantial shift in the role of the instructor (Cossom, 1991). The instructor no longer plays the role of the expert in charge of the classroom but rather a facilitator seeking to promote discussion and identifying linkages to concepts and principles. The instructor sets the intellectual tone of inquiry and serves as the stimulator of new ideas as well as the one who encourages visionary or alternative thinking (Webster, 1988). The following instructional practices can help create a learning environment in the classroom (Cossom,1991): 1) encourage learner input, 2) question and challenge students, 3) ask open-ended questions to stimulate discussion, 4) ask for clarification, 5) discourage quick-fix solutions, 6) assist in integrating case examples with theory and concepts, and 7) model active questioning and listening.

Selecting Cases

Instructors can choose cases for instructional purposes related to specific learning objectives by referring to 1) the brief case summary in the Table of Contents, 2) the discussion questions at the end of each case, and/or 3) the case matrix located in Appendix B. The matrix contains two components: the first displays a comprehensive listing of multiple intersecting issues, strengths, and challenges experienced by participants in the 20 cases, while the second notes the interventions and services that were provided in each case.

Case Reflection Strategies

Given the importance of self-reflective practice (Schon, 1983) and the content-specific questions found at the end of cases, instructors have an opportunity to teach students by utilizing different strategies with them to reflect critically on the cases. One of the major benefits of case-based learning is the opportunity for learners to refine and expand their critical thinking skills as noted in Figure A.1 (Gibbs & Gambrill, 1999). With regard to assessing complexity, Erskine, Leenders, and Mauffette-Leenders (1981) noted that the most difficult level of case-based learning involves cases in which a situation is described and learners are challenged to identify and prioritize the problems as well as formulate viable options/solutions. Yet, case debriefing is often a neglected aspect of case-based learning and teaching.

Using a Child Welfare Practice Framework

One of many possible case reflection strategies is illustrated in Figure A.2, Child Welfare Practice Framework for Case-Based Learning, that draws upon an adaptation of the California Core Practice Model for delivering public child welfare services. The five practice components noted in Figure A.2 represent a combination of the goals/outcomes of child welfare services as well as the relevant practice components that could be applied to any case. One approach to the use of the framework is in the form of a study guide. In this situation, learners are urged to complete the form after reading the case by placing their notes/observations in each cell PRIOR to group discussion. In this way, the instructor can focus on helping the participants to identify evidence buried in the case in order to reach a shared understanding of the

FIGURE A.1. Major Skill Sets in the Critical Thinking Process*

I. Clarifying—What is being stated?
  - Clarify problems
  - Clarify issues, conclusion, or beliefs
  - Identify unstated assumptions
  - Clarify and analyze the meanings of words and phrases
  - Clarify values and standards

II. Analyzing—What does it mean?
  - Identify significant similarities and differences
  - Recognize contradictions and inconsistencies
  - Analyze/evaluate arguments, interpretations, beliefs, or theories
  - Distinguish relevant from irrelevant questions, data, claims, or reasons
  - Detect bias
  - Evaluate the accuracy of different sources of information ("evidence")
  - Use sound criteria for evaluation
  - Compare perspectives, interpretations, or theories
  - Evaluate perspectives, interpretations, or theories

III. Applying—How can it be applied?
  - Compare with analogous situations; transfer insights to new contexts
  - Make well-reasoned inferences and predictions
  - Refine generalizations and avoid oversimplifications
  - Compare and contrast ideas with actual practice
  - Raise and pursue root or significant questions
  - Make interdisciplinary connections
  - Analyze or evaluate policies or actions

IV. Owning—How do the results of critical thinking apply to my situation?
  - Evaluate one's own reasoning process
  - Explore thoughts underlying feelings and feelings underlying thoughts
  - Design and carry out critical tests of concepts, theories, and hypotheses
  - Discover and accurately evaluate the implications and consequences of a proposed action

*Abstracted from "Examples of Critical Thinking Skills" (p 129), Gibbs, L & Gambrill, E. (1999) *Critical thinking for social workers.* Thousand Oaks, CA: Pine Forge Press.
Austin & Packard, http://www.tandfonline.com/toc/wtsw20/29/2?nav=tocList, pp. 229. Copyright © 2009 by Taylor & Francis Informa UK Ltd.

case. Then discussion can proceed to the identification of skillful practice and the rationale for making such judgments. The skill development underlying this form of structured learning can address one of the concerns raised in the past by juvenile court judges; namely, the lack of attention in court reports to clearly laying out the evidence in the case (away from statements that begin with "I feel" or "I believe") and the judgments required to delineate skillful intervention recommendations.

FIGURE A.2. Child Welfare Practice Framework for Case-based Learning*

Practice Components	Evidence of Each Practice Component Found in the Case	To What Extent Does this Evidence Reflect Skillful Practice?
1. ENGAGEMENT—listening to, and respecting to voice of families, tribes, youth, caregivers and communities in the assessment, planning and service delivery processes; approaching all interactions with openness, respect, and honesty, using understandable language, and describing our concerns clearly IN ORDER TO engage in inquiry and mutual exploration with the family to find, locate, and learn about other family members and supportive relationships children, youth, young adults, and families have within their communities and tribes and exploring with children, youth, and young adults their worries, wishes, where they feel safe, and consider their input about permanency and where they want to live.		
2. ASSESSMENT—a continuous process of discovery with families that leads to better understanding of the events and behaviors that brought the children and families into services IN ORDER TO plan and delivery services by working with the family and their team to create and tailor plans to build on the strengths and protective capacities of the youth and family members.		
3. TEAMWORK—working in partnership with families, communities, tribes, and other professionals and service providers and relying on their strength and support to help the family meet their underlying needs and, build an ongoing circle of support. This involves demonstrating respect, following through, and talking about and agreeing on team roles and team dynamics, including the role of supervisor/coach IN ORDER TO advocate for services, interventions, and supports that meet the needs of families, children, youth, and young adults and promoting the use of effective, available, evidence-informed, and culturally relevant services, interventions, and supports.		

(continued)

FIGURE A.2. (*Continued*)

Practice Components	Evidence of Each Practice Component Found in the Case	To What Extent Does this Evidence Reflect Skillful Practice?
4. MONITORING AND ADAPTING—the practice of continually monitoring and evaluating the effectiveness of the plan while assessing current circumstances and resources IN ORDER TO achieve positive outcomes for children, youth, young adults, and families in the areas of safety, permanency, and well-being involves measuring our practice against identified system goals and seeking continuous improvement (accountability)		
5. TRANSITION—the process of moving from formal supports and services to informal supports, when intervention by the formal systems is no longer needed IN ORDER TO focus on reducing risk factors and strengthening or increasing protective factors in families (prevention)		

*Adapted from:
California Social Work Education Center, California Child Welfare Core Practice Model, September 2016, retrieved from https://calswec.berkeley.edu/sites/default/files/cpm_packet_rev0816_p7.pdf

Developing Universal Discussion Questions

In addition to the specific discussion questions noted at the end of each case, a more universal set of case discussion questions could be developed based upon the knowledge and skill level of the learners.

Questions focusing on the child welfare system's response might include 1) In what ways did the child welfare system act in the best interests of the child?, 2) In what ways did the child welfare system lack the capacity to meet the needs of the child(ren) and family involved?, or 3) What material resource issues do you identify in the case, and how did these affect the family and child?

Questions focused on case documentation could include 1) After reviewing the case summary, can you identify any areas where our understanding of the situation might be incomplete or incorrect?, 2) Can you identify gaps or inconsistencies in the information gathered?, 3) How is this information important?, 4) How might this information have changed the outcome of the case?

Questions focused on the learner's assessment of what they gained from reviewing and reflecting on the case include 1) What is your reaction to the case description and practice challenges (easy, difficult, surprises, most meaningful part, etc.)?, 2) Can you identify any new learning for yourself (from the case itself, from the case discussion, from comparing the case with other cases, etc.)?, and 3) How might the learning from this case be applied to your own learning agenda (relevance to one's own experience, possibility of different outcomes in different organizational settings, major lessons learned)?

Questions and prompts related to self-assessment for bias could be framed as follows: In conducting assessments, it is important to be aware of your own beliefs, values, perceptions, and other underlying conditions that may have the potential to cause bias and may cause you to filter out information needed to make accurate assessments. 1) Identify your own negative reactions or biases toward this family. 2) How might you overcome these biases or assumptions?

Mapping the Child Welfare Policy and Practice Context
As was explained in the first two chapters, these are California-based cases. While some aspects of the child welfare system in California are unique to the state, other system components parallel service delivery models and practices in jurisdictions around the country A valuable learning activity for students could be to map aspects of the local child welfare context that would enable comparison with the practices described in these cases, and support reflection on implications for local practice. Potential strategies and sources for system mapping include 1) searching the website(s) of the state and/or county social service agencies to identify relevant policies, initiatives, and practice guidelines; 2) identifying any risk and safety assessment instruments used by child welfare agencies to inform decision-making; 3) reviewing the state's or county's System Improvement Plan developed for the federal Children and Family Services Review; 4) conducting legal research to identify state statutes and regulations that shape child welfare funding and practice; 5) identifying community-based organizations that engage in child welfare-related advocacy and services and reviewing reports, briefs, and other materials they produce related to the child welfare system; and 5) identifying the demographics of children, families, and foster parents who are involved in the child welfare system.

APPENDIX B
Matrix of Case Elements

In order to provide a summary overview of the cases, this matrix of case elements list key characteristics and interventions associated with the 20 cases. The case characteristics relate to the children and parents involved in the case, as well as the circumstances that brought the family to the attention of the child welfare agency. The case interventions relate to case planning and the services provided to the family. The matrix can be used to select cases for study that feature specific aspects of child welfare practice, and is organized into four sections: 1) Case characteristics for the first ten cases, 2) Service interventions for the first ten cases, 3) Case characteristics for the second ten cases, 4) Service interventions for the second ten cases.

CASE CHARACTERISTICS

	Calvin R	Tina C	Alex S	Donna S	Carlo M	Shawna L	Sean T	Lucia R	Jayden M	Caleb D
Absent Parent	X		X	X	X	X	X	X	X	
Absent Without Leave (AWOL)		X				X (Teen Parent)				
Adoption			X							
Allegation—General/ Severe Neglect	X			X		X	X	X	X	X
Allegation—Medical Neglect				X						
Allegation—Physical Abuse			X	X						
Allegation—Sexual Abuse		X								
Allegation—Emotional Abuse										
Case Manager					X					
Childcare Needs										

	Calvin R	Tina C	Alex S	Donna S	Carlo M	Shawna L	Sean T	Lucia R	Jayden M	Caleb D
Commercially Sexually Exploited Children (CSEC)		X				X			X	
Court Does Not Order CPS Recommendations								X	X	
Cultural Understanding		X					X			
Disability—Minor									X	
Disability—Parent			X							X
Domestic Violence	X	X	X	X	X	X		X	X	X
English as a Second Language		X					X	X		
Failure to Protect		X		X		X				
Gang Involvement—Minor		X								
Gang Involvement—Parent										
Guardianship										
Homeless	X				X		X			
Indian Child Welfare Act (ICWA)						X				

	Calvin R	Tina C	Alex S	Donna S	Carlo M	Shawna L	Sean T	Lucia R	Jayden M	Caleb D
Incarceration (Custody)—Parent		X		X	X			X	X	
Incarceration (Juvenile Hall)—Minor		X				X (Teen Parent)			X (Teen Parent)	
Maltreatment in Foster Care	X									
Medical Marijuana Card										
Mental Health—Minor	X	X	X		X		X			
Mental Health—Minor Hospitalized		X								
Mental Health—Parent	X	X				X		X	X	X
Mental Health—Parent Hospitalized									X	
Minor—Behavior Disruptive		X	X				X	X		
Minor—Teen		X	X							
Minor—Teen Parent						X			X	
Minor—Under 3				X	X	X		X	X	X

	Calvin R	Tina C	Alex S	Donna S	Carlo M	Shawna L	Sean T	Lucia R	Jayden M	Caleb D
Minor Afraid to Return Home										
Minor Parent						X			X	
Minor Sexually Acting Out										
Non-Offending Parent	X									
Parent Abused as Child						X		X		
Parent Out of State			X							
Parole								X		
Paternity—Undetermined	X					X		X		
Placement—3 or more	X	X	X	X	X	X	X		X	
Placement—Foster Family Agency (FFA)	X	X	X	X	X	X	X	X	X	
Placement—Group Home		X								
Placement—Out of County						X (Teen Parent)			X (Teen Parent)	
Placement—Relative/Kinship	X	X	X	X	X	X	X	X	X	X

	Calvin R	Tina C	Alex S	Donna S	Carlo M	Shawna L	Sean T	Lucia R	Jayden M	Caleb D
Placement—Relative/Kinship Exemption	X									
Placement—Relative/Kinship Not Approved					X			X	X	X
Placement—Relative/Kinship Funding					X					
Placement Concerns			X		X	X			X	X
Pos Tox					X					
Pregnant Parent				X	X		X		X	
Prior CPS Contact	X	X	X	X				X		X
Probation—Minor		X				X (Teen Parent)				
Probation—Parent					X	X (Teen Parent)				
Registered Sexual Offender in the Home				X						
Restraining Order/No Contact Order				X	X	X			X	
School—Special Education (IEP/504)		X			X		X			

	Calvin R	Tina C	Alex S	Donna S	Carlo M	Shawna L	Sean T	Lucia R	Jayden M	Caleb D
School Issues/Concerns		X	X							
Self-Harm		X								
Sexual Abuse		X								
Sexually Acting Out				X						
Sibling Set	X	X			X		X	X		X
Sibling Set—Sibling Under 3							X			X
Social Security Benefits—Minor			X							
Social Security Benefits—Parent										
Social Worker—Threatened		X	X							
Social Worker Change										
Substance Abuse—Minor		X				X				
Substance Abuse—Parent	X	X	X		X			X	X	X
Suicidal—Minor		X								

	Calvin R	Tina C	Alex S	Donna S	Carlo M	Shawna L	Sean T	Lucia R	Jayden M	Caleb D
Suicidal—Parent										
Transitional Housing/Sober Living	X		X							
Truancy			X							
Undocumented Minor or Parent					X					
Unemployment	X									X

CASE INTERVENTIONS

	Calvin R	Tina C	Alex S	Donna S	Carlo M	Shawna L	Sean T	Lucia R	Jayden M	Caleb D
12-Step Program				X	X					
AA/NA/Al-Anon		X		X						X
Adoption	X		X	X		X	X	X	X	X
Assessment Center	X	X	X	X			X		X (Teen Parent)	
Bypass Parent		X	X					X		
Case Plan—Parent Not Engaged	X	X			X	X	X		X	X
Case Plan Change	X								X	
Case Plan Services—Conflict with Work		X						X		X
Case Plan Services—Did Not Meet Needs										X
Commercially Sexually Exploited Children (CSEC)		X								
Concurrent Plan				X	X	X		X	X	X
Court Appointed Special Advocate (CASA)		X					X			

	Calvin R	Tina C	Alex S	Donna S	Carlo M	Shawna L	Sean T	Lucia R	Jayden M	Caleb D
Cultural Understanding		X								
Detox	X		X							
Documentation—Good								X		X
Documentation—Poor	X						X	X	X	X
Domestic Violence—52-Week Program					X			X		
Drug Testing	X	X	X	X	X	X	X	X	X	X
DUI Class										
Extended Family Involvement	X	X	X		X	X	X		X	X
Family (Parent) Advocate		X		X						
Family Finding	X		X	X						X
Family Maintenance		X		X	X				X	X
Family Maintenance—Over 12 Months										
Family Maintenance—Over 24 Months										
Family Reunification					X					

	Calvin R	Tina C	Alex S	Donna S	Carlo M	Shawna L	Sean T	Lucia R	Jayden M	Caleb D
Family Reunification Services—Over 12 Months				X	X		X			
Family Reunification Services—Over 18 Months										
Family Reunification Services—Over 24 Months										
Family Reunification Services—Over 6 Months (Under 3)					X	X			X	
Family Reunification Services Terminated	X	X	X		X	X	X	X	X	
Family Therapy		X		X			X			
Father Involvement	X		X	X	X	X	X	X		X
Financial Assistance		X		X	X				X	
Forensic Interview		X								
Guardianship	X						X		X	
In-Home Services			X							X

	Calvin R	Tina C	Alex S	Donna S	Carlo M	Shawna L	Sean T	Lucia R	Jayden M	Caleb D
Linkages/CalWORKs					X					
Mentor			X							
Other Planned Permanent Living Arrangement (OPPLA)			X				X			
Parent/Child Therapy				X				X		
Parental Rights Terminated			X			X		X	X	X
Parenting Classes/Education	X						X	X		
Safety Plan				X						X
School—Educational Rights Limited/Surrogate		X							X	
School Counselor/Therapy	X	X	X							
Social Worker Engagement		X		X			X		X	
Substance Abuse Treatment—Outpatient	X				X					X

	Calvin R	Tina C	Alex S	Donna S	Carlo M	Shawna L	Sean T	Lucia R	Jayden M	Caleb D
Substance Abuse Treatment—Residential/Inpatient	X							X		X
Team Meeting	X	X	X	X	X	X	X		X	X
Visitation—Extended Home Visit										
Visitation—Supervised—Family/Kinship	X				X					
Visitation—Supervised—Foster Parent	X									
Visitation—Supervised—Social Worker				X						
Visitation—Supervised—Visitation Center	X			X					X	X
Visitation—Therapeutic				X					X	
Wrap				X						

CASE CHARACTERISTICS

	Anthony R	Lila S	Brandon B	Marilyn K	Ronald R	Sophia W	Nathan D	James T	Mason T	Noah M
Absent Parent		X		X			X			X
Absent Without Leave (AWOL)									X	
Adoption					X					
Allegation—General/Severe Neglect										
Allegation—Medical Neglect		X	X		X	X		X		
Allegation—Physical Abuse										
Allegation—Sexual Abuse	X					X	X		X	
Allegation—Emotional Abuse										X
Case Manager						X				
Childcare Needs			X					X	X	
Commercially Sexually Exploited Children (CSEC)										

	Anthony R	Lila S	Brandon B	Marilyn K	Ronald R	Sophia W	Nathan D	James T	Mason T	Noah M
Court Does Not Order CPS Recommendations										
Cultural Understanding										
Disability—Minor										
Disability—Parent							X			
Domestic Violence	X	X	X	X		X	X	X		X
English as a Second Language										
Failure to Protect	X								X	X
Gang Involvement—Minor		X								
Gang Involvement—Parent										
Guardianship										
Homeless		X	X	X			X		X	
ICWA										
Incarceration (Custody)—Parent	X	X	X			X	X		X	X
Incarceration (Juvenile Hall)—Minor									X	

	Anthony R	Lila S	Brandon B	Marilyn K	Ronald R	Sophia W	Nathan D	James T	Mason T	Noah M
Maltreatment in Foster Care					X					
Medical Marijuana Card	X							X		
Mental Health—Minor					X				X	
Mental Health—Minor Hospitalized									X	X
Mental Health—Parent					X				X	
Mental Health—Parent Hospitalized			X	X		X	X			X
MI's Behavior Disruptive	X				X	X				
Minor—Teen									X	
Minor—Teen Parent										
Minor—Under 3										
Minor Afraid to Return Home	X									
Minor Parent										
Minor Sexually Acting Out										

	Anthony R	Lila S	Brandon B	Marilyn K	Ronald R	Sophia W	Nathan D	James T	Mason T	Noah M
Non-Offending Parent		X				X				
Parent Abused as Child						X				
Parent Out of State										
Parole		X				X				
Paternity—Undetermined		X								
Placement—3 or more			X		X	X			X	
Placement—Foster Family Agency (FFA)	X	X	X	X	X	X			X	
Placement—Group Home									X	
Placement—Out of County					X				X	
Placement—Relative/Kinship	X	X	X	X			X			
Placement—Relative/Kinship Exemption							X			
Placement—Relative/Kinship Not Approved		X								
Placement—Relative/Kinship Funding		X					X			

	Anthony R	Lila S	Brandon B	Marilyn K	Ronald R	Sophia W	Nathan D	James T	Mason T	Noah M
Placement Concerns					X					
Pos Tox										
Pregnant Parent										
Prior CPS Contact	X		X	X	X		X	X	X	X
Probation—Minor										
Probation—Parent			X							
Registered Sexual Offender in the Home										
Restraining Order/No Contact	X	X	X				X	X	X	X
School—Special Education (IEP/504)					X				X	
School Issues/Concerns	X			X	X	X	X	X	X	
Self-Harm										
Sexual Abuse										
Sexually Acting Out										
Sibling Set		X	X		X	X			X	X
Sibling Set—Sibling Under 3		X	X							

	Anthony R	Lila S	Brandon B	Marilyn K	Ronald R	Sophia W	Nathan D	James T	Mason T	Noah M
Social Security Benefits—Minor										
Social Security Benefits—Parent										
Social Worker—Threatened										
Social Worker Change	X				X					
Substance Abuse—Minor						X			X	
Substance Abuse—Parent	X	X	X	X		X	X	X		X
Suicidal—Minor									X	
Suicidal—Parent							X			
Transitional Housing/Sober Living				X						
Truancy										
Undocumented Minor or Parent										
Unemployment		X		X		X				

CASE INTERVENTIONS

	Anthony R	Lila S	Brandon B	Marilyn K	Ronald R	Sophia W	Nathan D	James T	Mason T	Noah M
12-Step Program	X			X		X				
AA/NA/Al-Anon						X				
Adoption		X	X				X			
Assessment Center				X	X		X		X	
Bypass Parent				X						
Case Plan—Parent Not Engaged	X	X				X		X	X	
Case Plan Change						X		X	X	
Case Plan Services—Conflict with Work			X							
Case Plan Services—Did Not Meet Needs						X				X
Commercially Sexually Exploited Children (CSEC)										
Concurrent Plan		X			X					
Court Appointed Special Advocate (CASA)									X	

	Anthony R	Lila S	Brandon B	Marilyn K	Ronald R	Sophia W	Nathan D	James T	Mason T	Noah M
Cultural Understanding										
Detox		X					X			
Documentation—Good										
Documentation—Poor			X				X			
Domestic Violence—52-Week Program	X	X					X			X
Drug Testing	X	X	X	X		X		X	X	
DUI Class			X			X				
Extended Family Involvement		X	X		X	X	X	X	X	X
Family (Parent) Advocate			X							X
Family Finding	X			X	X		X			
Family Maintenance	X		X	X	X	X		X	X	X
Family Maintenance—Over 12 Months								X	X	X
Family Maintenance—Over 24 Months									X	
Family Reunification	X		X			X				

	Anthony R	Lila S	Brandon B	Marilyn K	Ronald R	Sophia W	Nathan D	James T	Mason T	Noah M
Family Reunification Services—Over 12 Months	X			X	X	X			X	
Family Reunification Services—Over 18 Months							X			
Family Reunification Services—Over 24 Months									X	
Family Reunification Services—Over 6 Months (Under 3)										
Family Reunification Services Terminated	X	X	X				X		X	X
Family Therapy		X	X		X	X	X			X
Father Involvement			X			X				
Financial Assistance		X	X			X		X	X	
Forensic Interview										
Guardianship		X			X		X			
In-Home Services		X	X		X				X	
Linkages/CalWORKs						X	X			

	Anthony R	Lila S	Brandon B	Marilyn K	Ronald R	Sophia W	Nathan D	James T	Mason T	Noah M
Mentor										
Other Planned Permanent Living Arrangement (OPPLA)										
Parent/Child Therapy			X							
Parental Rights Terminated		X		X (Prior CPS Case—Siblings)						
Parenting Classes/Education	X	X	X		X	X			X	
Safety Plan	X					X				X
School—Educational Rights Limited/Surrogate							X			
School Counselor/Therapy										
Social Worker Engagement	X	X		X		X			X	X
Substance Abuse Treatment—Outpatient			X	X			X			X

	Anthony R	Lila S	Brandon B	Marilyn K	Ronald R	Sophia W	Nathan D	James T	Mason T	Noah M
Substance Abuse Treatment—Residential/Inpatient			X	X		X	X			X
Team Meeting		X	X	X	X	X	X	X		X
Visitation—Extended Home Visit	X		X	X						
Visitation—Supervised—Family/Kinship							X			
Visitation—Supervised—Foster Parent		X								
Visitation—Supervised—Social Worker										
Visitation—Supervised—Visitation Center		X				X				
Visitation—Therapeutic	X			X					X	
Wrap					X					

Casebook References

CHAPTER 1

Administration for Children and Families (ACF). (2012). *Information memorandum: Establishing and maintaining continuous quality improvement (CQI) systems in state child welfare agencies.* Retrieved from https://www.acf.hhs.gov/sites/default/files/cb/im1207.pdf

Administration for Children and Families (ACF). (2016). *Child and Family Services Reviews: Statewide assessment instrument, California, March 25, 2016.*

Baird, C., & Wagner, D. (2000). The relative validity of actuarial- and consensus-based risk assessment systems. *Children and Youth Services Review, 22,* 839–871.

California Department of Social Services (CDSS). (2014). *California Child and Family Services Review instruction manual.* Retrieved from http://www.cdss.ca.gov/Portals/9/CCFSRInstructionManual.pdf?ver=2017-10-03-090658-660

California Department of Social Services (CDSS). (2015). *California Department of Social Services—2015-2019 Child and Family Services Plan.* Retrieved from http://www.childsworld.ca.gov/res/TitleIV-B/CFSP_2015-2019.pdf

California Department of Social Services (CDSS). (2016). *Child and Family Services Plan 2015-2019: Annual progress and services report, June 30, 2016.*

California Department of Social Services (CDSS). (2018). *California-Child and Family Services Review (C-CFSR).* Retrieved from http://www.cdss.ca.gov/inforesources/Child-Welfare-Program-Improvement/Child-and-Family-Services-Review

California Social Work Education Center (CalSWEC). (2016). *California Child Welfare Core Practice Model.* Retrieved from https://calswec.berkeley.edu/sites/default/files/cpm_packet_rev0816_p7.pdf

Carnochan, S., Rizik-Baer, D., & Austin, M. J. (2013). Preventing the recurrence of maltreatment. *Journal of Evidence-Based Social Work, 10*(3), 161–178.

Children's Bureau. (2014). Permanency Innovations Initiative (PII) project resources. Retrieved from https://www.acf.hhs.gov/cb/resource/pii-project-resources

Children's Bureau. (2015). Child and Family Services Reviews fact sheet. Retrieved from https://www.acf.hhs.gov/sites/default/files/cb/cfsr_general_factsheet.pdf

Dorsey, S., Mustillo, S. S., Farmer, E. M. Z., & Elbogen, E. (2008). Caseworker assessments of risk for recurrent maltreatment: Association with case-specific factors and re-reports. *Child Abuse & Neglect, 32*(3), 377–391.

Hernandez, V. R. (2017). *Message from Executive Director Virginia Rondero Hernandez, CalSWEC News, May – August 2017.* California Social Work Education Center. Retrieved from https://calswec.berkeley.edu/news/may-2017-california-child-welfare-core-practice-model-overview

King, B., Needell, B., Dawson, B., Webster, D., & Magruder, J. (2015). *CFSR3 data overview.* Berkeley, CA: Child Welfare Indicators Project.

Meitner, H., & Albers, M. (2012). *Introducing Safety-Organized Practice*. National Council on Crime and Delinquency, Children's Research Center (NCCD/CRC). Retrieved from http://bayareaacademy.org/wp-content/uploads/2013/05/SOP-Handout-Booklet-9-20-12.pdf

National Child Welfare Resource Center for Organizational Improvement and Casey Family Programs (NCWRC/CFP). (2005). *Using Continuous Quality Improvement to improve child welfare practice: A framework for implementation*. Retrieved from http://muskie.usm.maine.edu/helpkids/rcpdfs/cqiframework.pdf

National Child Welfare Resource Center for Organizational Improvement and National Resource Center for Family Centered Practice and Permanency Planning (NCWRC/NRC). (July 2008). *An introduction to the Practice Model Framework: A working document series*. Retrieved from http://muskie.usm.maine.edu/helpkids/practicemodel/PracticeModelWorkingPaperIntro.pdf

National Council on Crime and Delinquency, Children's Research Center (NCCD/CRC). (2015). *The Structured Decision Making System, policy and procedure manual, SDM 3.0*. Retrieved from http://www.childsworld.ca.gov/res/pdf/SDM_Manual.pdf

Reed, D. F., & Karpilow, K. (2009). *Understanding the child welfare system in California: A primer for service providers and policymakers*. Oakland, CA: California Center for Research on Women and Families/Public Health Institute. Retrieved from http://www.phi.org/uploads/application/files/h31ef4xly0mtt9oa4lsv07oko48r6kg19g6fisdm62qmymwbs5.pdf

Rossi, P. H., Schuerman, I., & Budde, S. (1996). *Understanding child maltreatment decisions and those who make them*. Chicago, IL: Chapin Hall at the University of Chicago.

Rossi, P. H., Schuerman, I., & Budde, S. (1999). Understanding decisions about child maltreatment. *Evaluation Review, 23*, 579–598.

79 Federal Register (FR) 61241, October 10, 2014. Retrieved from https://www.federalregister.gov/documents/2014/10/10/2014-24204/statewide-data-indicators-and-national-standards-for-child-and-family-services-reviews

Spar, K., & Shuman, M. (2004). *Child welfare: Implementation of the Adoption and Safe Families Act (P. L. 105-89)*. Washington, DC: Congressional Research Service. Retrieved from https://greenbook-waysandmeans.house.gov/sites/greenbook.waysandmeans.house.gov/files/2012/RL30759_gb.pdf

Webster, D., Armijo, M., Lee, S., Dawson, W., Magruder, J., Exel, M..., & Cotto, H. (2017). *CCWIP reports*. Berkeley, CA: Child Welfare Indicators Project. Retrieved from http://cssr.berkeley.edu/ucb_childwelfare/PIT.aspx

CHAPTER 2

Ames, N. (1999). Social work recording: A new look at an old issue. *Journal of Social Work Education, 35*(2), 227–238.

Askeland, G. A., & Payne, M. (2001). *What is valid knowledge for social workers?* Retrieved from http://brage.bibsys.no/xmlui/handle/11250/98971

Austin, M. J., & Packard, T. (2009). Case-based learning: Educating future human service managers. *Journal of Teaching in Social Work, 29*(2), 216–236.

Birren, J. E. & Fisher, L. M. (1990). The elements of wisdom: Overview and integration. In R.J. Sternberg (Ed.), *Wisdom: Its nature, origins, and development* (pp. 317–332). Cambridge University Press.

Carnochan, S., Weissinger, E., Henry, C., Liner-Jigamian, N., & Austin, M. J. (2018). Identifying skillful practice in child welfare case record data using qualitative data mining. *Journal of Public Child Welfare, 93*(6), 1—22.

Cumming, S., Fitzpatrick, E., McAuliffe, D., McKain, S., Martin, C., & Tonge, A. (2007). Raising the Titanic: Rescuing social work documentation from the sea of ethical risk. *Australian Social Work, 60*(2), 239–257.

DePanfilis, D., & Salus, M. K. (2003). *Child protective services: A guide for caseworkers.* Washington, DC: U.S. Dept. of Health and Human Services, Administration for Children and Families, Administration on Children, Youth and Families, Children's Bureau, Office on Child Abuse and Neglect.

Garrett, K. J. (2012). Managing school social work records. *Children & Schools, 34*(4), 239–248. http://doi.org/10.1093/cs/cds003

Gelman, S. B. (1992). Risk management through client access to case records. *Social Work, 37*(1), 73.

Henry, C., Carnochan, S., & Austin, M. J. (2014). Using qualitative data-mining for practice research in child welfare. *Child Welfare, 93*(6), 7–26.

Henry, C., Liner-Jigamian, N., Carnochan, S., Taylor, S., & Austin, M. J. (2018). Parental substance use: How child welfare workers make the case for juvenile court intervention. *Children and Youth Services Review, 93*, 69—78

Kagle, J. D. (1983). The contemporary social work record. *Social Work, 28*(2), 149–153.

Kagle, J. D., & Kopels, S. (2008). *Social work records* (3rd ed.). Long Grove, IL: Waveland Press.

Khoo, E. G., & Umeå universitet. (2004). *Protecting our children: A comparative study of the dynamics of structure, intervention and their interplay in Swedish child welfare and Canadian child protection.* Umeå: Umeå University. Retrieved from http://urn.kb.se/resolve?urn=urn:nbn:se:umu:diva-193

Klein, W. C. & Bloom, M. (1995). Practice wisdom. *Social Work, 40*(6), 799–807.

Martin, E., & Moriarty, R. (2012). An exploratory examination of record keeping policies and procedures in preparation for evidence-based practice. *Administration in Social Work, 36*(5), 520–544.

McDevitt, S. (1994). Case records in public child welfare: Uses and a flexible format. *Child Welfare, 73*(1), 41.

Murray, S., & Humphreys, C. (2014). "My life's been a total disaster but I feel privileged": Care-leavers' access to personal records and their implications for social work practice. *Child & Family Social Work, 19*(2), 215–224.

Reamer, F. G. (2005). Documentation in social work: Evolving ethical and risk-management standards. *Social Work, 50*(4), 325–334.

Reilly, S., McKelvey-Walsh, N., Freundlich, M., & Brenner, E. (2011). Training and technology: Improving the quality and timeliness of service plans and case documentation. *Administration in Social Work, 35*(2), 207–222.

Stephenson-Valcourt, D. (2009–2010). From the practitioner's desk: Documenting case notes in child welfare: The 8-frame window. *Illinois Child Welfare, 5*(1), 162–168.

Taylor, S., Battis, C., Carnochan, S., Henry, C., Balk, M., & Austin, M. J. (2018). Exploring trauma-informed practice in public child welfare through qualitative data mining of case records. *Journal of Public Child Welfare*, 1—20.

Zeira, A. (2014). Training social workers to understand and use evidence. In A. Shlonsky and R. Benbenishty (Eds.), *From evidence to outcomes in child welfare: An international reader* (pp. 161–170). Oxford: Oxford University Press.

CHAPTER 3

Brewer, L. K., Roditti, M., & Marcus, A. (1996). Child welfare case study module: Emergency response, family maintenance, permanency planning. Berkeley: University of California at Berkeley, California Social Work Education Center. Retrieved from http://web.csulb.edu/projects/ccwrl/Child%20Welfare%20Case%20Study%20Module.pdf

APPENDIX A

Altshuler, S., & Bosch, L. (2003). Problem-based learning in social work education. *Journal of Teaching Social Work*, 23(1/2), 201–215.

Austin, M. J., & Packard, T. (2009). Case-based learning: Educating future human service managers. *Journal of Teaching in Social Work*, 29(2), 216–236.

Cossom, J. (1991). Teaching from cases: Education for critical thinking. *Journal of Teaching Social Work*, 5(1), 139–155.

Erskine, J., Leenders, M., & Mauffette-Leenders, L. (1981). *Teaching with cases* (3rd ed.). London, Ontario: Ivey Publishing.

Ferguson, K. (2005). Problem-based learning: Let's not throw the baby out with the bath-water. *Medical Education*, 39, 350–355.

Gibbs, L. & Gambrill, E. (1999). *Critical thinking for social workers*. Thousand Oaks, CA: Pine Forge Press.

Jones, K. (2003). Making the case for the case method in graduate social work education. *Journal of Teaching Social Work*, 23(1/2), 183–197.

Kimball, B. (1995). *The emergence of case method teaching, 1870s–1990s: A search for legitimate pedagogy*. Bloomington, IN: The Pointer Center for the Study of Ethics and American Institutions, Indiana University.

Lynn, L. (1999). *Teaching and learning with cases: A guidebook*. New York: Chatham House Publishers.

Schon, D. (1983). *The reflective practitioner*. New York: New York Basic Books.

Wassermann, S. (1994). *Introduction to case method teaching: A guide to the galaxy*. New York: Teachers College Press.

Webster, W. (1988). Student-developed case studies. *College Teaching*, 36(Winter), 25–27.

Glossary

504 Supportive Services

Minors

A student with a disability under Section 504 is one who has a physical or mental impairment (e.g., diabetes, asthma, bipolar disorder, etc.) that substantially limits one or more major life activities. Major life activities include, but are not limited to, caring for oneself, performing manual tasks, walking, seeing, hearing, speaking, breathing, learning, and working.

Adapted from: https://www.alameda.k12.ca.us/studentservices#Section504

Parents

Section 504 of the Rehabilitation Act of 1973 (Section 504) and Title II of the Americans with Disabilities Act of 1990 (ADA) protect parents and prospective parents with disabilities from unlawful discrimination in the administration of child welfare programs, activities, and services. Child welfare agencies are required to ensure that parents and prospective parents with disabilities involved in the child welfare system are afforded an opportunity to preserve their families and/or to become parents that is equal to the opportunity that the entities offer to individuals without disabilities. Service plans for parents and prospective parents should address the individual's disability-related needs and the auxiliary aids and services the agency will provide to ensure equal opportunities. At the same time, service plans should not rely on fears or stereotypes to require parents with disabilities to accept unnecessary services or complete unnecessary tasks to prove their fitness to parent when nondisabled parents would not be required to do so.

Adapted from: https://www.ada.gov/doj_hhs_ta/child_welfare_ta.html

Alternate/Other Permanent Planned Living Arrangement

ASFA replaced the term "long-term foster care" with "other planned permanent living arrangement" (OPPLA) and "another planned permanent living arrangement" (APPLA). Under OPPLA, the child welfare agency retains care and custody of the youth and arranges a living situation that is expected to last until the youth reaches adulthood. OPPLA or APPLA becomes the permanency option only when other options have been ruled out.

Adapted from: https://www.childwelfare.gov/topics/outofhome/foster-care/oppla-appla/

Alternative Response/Differential Response

Alternative or Differential Response (DR) is a strategy that allows a California child welfare services (CWS) agency to respond more flexibly to reports of child abuse or neglect based on an assessment of safety, risk, and protective capacity that recognizes each family's unique strengths and needs and address these in an individualized manner. DR has three referral paths, which are assigned by the social worker based on information taken from the initial report:

Path 1—Community Response
When the allegations do not meet statutory definitions of abuse or neglect, but the family is experiencing problems and is therefore linked to voluntary services such as counseling, parenting classes, or other supportive options to strengthen the family.

Path 2—Child Welfare Services and Agency Partners Response
When the allegations meet statutory definitions of abuse and neglect at low to moderate risk and assessments indicate that a family is likely to make needed progress to improve child safety and mitigate risk with targeted services provided through multidisciplinary teamwork between CWS and interagency or community partners.

Path 3—Child Welfare Services Response
When initial assessment indicates the child is not safe, the child welfare system employs its traditional response.

> *Adapted from: http://www.cdss.ca.gov/inforesources/Child-Welfare-Protection/*
> *Differential-Response*

AWOL
AWOL is an acronym for absent without leave. The term refers to youth running away from out-of-home placement.

> *Adapted from: https://theacademy.sdsu.edu/pcwtacurriculum/*
> *understanding-and-managing-awol-behaviors-in-out-of-home-placement/*

Background Check
In California, the following persons or entities are required to have records checks:
- Applicants for licensure or approval to provide direct care services in a community care facility, foster family home, or a certified family home of a licensed Foster Family Agency
- Any person, other than a client, residing in the facility or certified family home
- Any staff person, volunteer, or employee who has contact with the clients
- Any prospective licensed or certified foster parent, adoptive parent, or any person age 18 or older residing in the household
- A person seeking licensure or approval to operate or provide direct care services in a childcare center or family childcare home

Records checks also are required as part of an abbreviated adoption home study assessment for any of the following:
- A licensed or certified foster parent with whom the child has lived for a minimum of six months

- An approved relative caregiver or nonrelated extended family member with whom the child has had an ongoing and significant relationship
- A court-appointed relative guardian of the child who has been investigated and approved pursuant to the guardianship investigation process and has had physical custody of the child for at least one year
- A prospective adoptive parent who has completed an agency-supervised adoption within the last two years

Adapted from: https://www.childwelfare.gov/pubPDFs/background.
pdf#page=5&view=Summaries%20of%20State%20laws

Behavioral/Educational Surrogate

If the court cannot locate a responsible adult for the child and the child has been referred to the LEA (local educational agency) for special education or has an IEP, the court must refer the child to the LEA for appointment of a "surrogate parent." The LEA must select a relative caretaker, foster parent, or court-appointed special advocate (CASA) if one is willing and able to serve. A surrogate parent may represent an individual with exceptional needs in matters relating to identification, assessment, instructional planning and development, educational placement, reviewing and revising the IEP, and in other matters related to the provision of a free appropriate public education to the individual.

Adapted from: http://www.cfyetf.org/publications_19_421458854.pdf

Bypass

Bypass refers to the authority of the juvenile court under ASFA and California's Welfare & Institutions Code § 361.5(b) to allow the child welfare agency not to provide reunification services to a parent when specific circumstances related to increased risk or harm or criminal conduct are present.

Adapted from: http://cadependencyonlineguide.info/view/articles/11986.pdf

CalWORKs

CalWORKs is a public assistance program (based on the federal Temporary Assistance to Needy Families–TANF) that provides cash aid and employment and other services to eligible families that have children in the home. The program serves all 58 counties in the state and is operated by county welfare departments at the local level.

Adapted from: http://www.cdss.ca.gov/CalWORKs

Caregiver/Relative Approval and Exemptions

When children are placed in a home, a background check is conducted of the applicant and all adults regularly residing in the home. This background check includes, but is not limited to, the following reviews/searches: state and federal criminal records, Child Abuse Central Index (CACI), registration as sexual offender, DMV, CDSS's Administrative Action Records System (AARS) and Notice of Action (NOA) databases, and Licensing Information System (LIS) database for previous licensing and criminal records exemption history. If the background check reveals a criminal record for the applicant and/or another adult living in the home, the applicant may be able to obtain a criminal records exemption.

Adapted from: https://www.advokids.org/resource-family-approval-rfa-program/

Case Plan

Since the passage of the Adoption Assistance and Child Welfare Act (P.L. 96-272) in 1980, federal law requires the development of a written case plan for any child receiving foster care maintenance payments under title IV-E. California also requires a case plan when a child and his or her family are receiving any kind of in-home services to prevent placement or when the child has been placed in the legal custody of the state agency.

Adapted from: https://www.childwelfare.gov/pubPDFs/caseplanning.pdf

Commercially Sexually Exploited Child (CSEC)

Defined as the sexual abuse of a minor entirely, or at least primarily, for financial or other economic reasons. The economic exchanges involved may be either monetary or non-monetary (e.g., food, shelter, drugs). Within the United States, California has emerged as a magnet for sex trafficking of children.

Adapted from: http://www.chhs.ca.gov/Child%20Welfare/CSEC%20Fact%20Sheet%20-%201.pdf.

Concurrent Plan/Concurrent Planning

Concurrent planning, required by the Adoption and Safe Families Act of 1997, is an approach that seeks to eliminate delays in attaining permanent families for children and youth in foster care. It involves identifying and working toward a child's primary permanency goal (such as reunification with the birth family) while simultaneously identifying and working on a secondary goal (such as guardianship with a relative).

Adapted from: https://www.childwelfare.gov/topics/permanency/planning/concurrent/

County Assessment Center

Some counties have assessment centers that are utilized to screen, assess, and house children for less than 24 hours while a placement is located. Case records may also refer to emergency children's shelter.

Adapted from: http://hs.sbcounty.gov/cfs/Documents/Annual%20report.pdf;
https://www.sandiegocounty.gov/content/dam/sdc/hhsa/programs/cs/documents/San_Diego_2011_CSA_Report.pdf

Court Hearings

Detention Hearing

At the detention hearing, parents are provided with notice of the proceedings, a copy of the petition, and supporting documents. Attorneys representing the parties are identified. Relatives and paternity may also be identified at this hearing. The court determines whether the child should remain with a parent or be placed outside of home until the disposition hearing. If the child is removed from a parent, the court issues visitation orders, refers the parents to services, and determines whether the agency has made reasonable efforts to prevent removal of the child from his or her parent(s).

Jurisdiction Hearing

The court determines whether the statements in the petition are true based upon an admission by the parents or guardians, a submission by the parents or guardians, or after a contested hearing at which evidence is presented to the court.

Disposition Hearing

At the disposition hearing, the court decides whether to 1) dismiss the proceedings; 2) place the child with a parent on family maintenance; 3) remove the child from the parents and place with a relative, foster parent, or in a group home and offer the parents family reunification services; or 4) remove the child from the parents and not offer the parents family reunification services.

In some situations, the court may *bypass* family reunification services and order a permanency planning hearing. The decision to bypass services may be based upon the following circumstances:

1. The child or a sibling was seriously abused or killed
2. The parent has had another child removed by the court
3. Family reunification services have previously been terminated
4. The parent has a serious substance abuse problem

Six-Month Status Review Hearing

At the six-month status review hearing, the court reviews 1) the child's progress in his/her current placement and 2) the parents' progress . If the child is living with a parent, the court may decide to continue to provide court supervision under family maintenance or dismiss the case. If the child is in out-of-home care, the court may decide to continue out-of-home care and family reunification services or return the child to a parent with family maintenance services.

Twelve-Month Status Review Hearing

At the 12-month status review hearing the court decides whether the child will return to the parents or services will be terminated and a permanency plan developed for the child. The court will extend services for an additional six months only if there is a substantial probability that family reunification can take place within that time frame. If not, family reunification services will be terminated and a hearing will be set to determine a permanency plan for the child.

Eighteen-Month Status Review Hearing

At the 18-month status review hearing, the court decides whether the child will be returned to the parents or whether services will be terminated and a hearing scheduled to determine the permanency plan.

Adapted from: http://www.courts.ca.gov/documents/Dependency_Flow_chart.pdf. See also http://www.alameda.courts.ca.gov/Pages.aspx/Dependency-Legal-Hearings

366.26 Selection and Implementation Hearing

If the time for reunification services has expired and the parent or guardian has failed to reunify with the child, the court must terminate any further reunification services and set a hearing pursuant to section 366.26 of the Welfare and Institutions Code. The 366.26 hearing, also known as a selection and implementation hearing, must occur within 120 days of the order terminating reunification services. At the conclusion of the hearing the court determines whether adoption, legal guardianship, or a planned permanent living arrangement is the most appropriate plan.

Adapted from: http://www.courts.ca.gov/documents/CIPReassessmentRpt.pdf

Contested Hearing

Rule 5.684. Contested hearing on petition

(a) Contested jurisdiction hearing (§ 355)

If the parent or guardian denies the allegations of the petition, the court must hold a contested hearing and determine whether the allegations in the petition are true.

Source: 2018 California Rules of Court http://www.courts.ca.gov/cms/rules/index. cfm?title=five&linkid=rule5_684

Continuance/Continued Hearing

The court may order a continuance of the hearing if requested to do so by the attorney for the parent, guardian, child, or the department as long as the continuance is not contrary to the interest of the child (WIC § 352). In order for a continuance to be granted, there must be a showing of good cause and it may only be for that period of time shown to be necessary by the evidence presented at the hearing on the motion for the continuance.

Adapted from: https://www.sccgov.org/ssa/opp2/08_juvenilecourt/8-4.html

WIC 352 (a): Upon request of counsel for the parent, guardian, minor, or petitioner, the court may continue any hearing under this chapter beyond the time limit within which the hearing is otherwise required to be held, provided that no continuance shall be granted that is contrary to the interest of the minor. In considering the minor's interests, the court shall give substantial weight to a minor's need for prompt resolution of his or her custody status, the need to provide children with stable environments, and the damage to a minor of prolonged temporary placements. Continuances shall be granted only upon a showing of good cause and only for that period of time shown to be necessary by the evidence presented at the hearing on the motion for the continuance.

Source: https://codes.findlaw.com/ca/welfare-and-institutions-code/wic-sect-352.html

Interim Review Hearing

The status of a child in foster care must be reviewed no less frequently than once every six months as calculated from the date of the original disposition hearing. In addition to mandated periodic review hearings, many courts regularly hold non-statutory interim review hearings to check the status of, or progress on, a variety of issues, such as visitation, participation in case plan services, and relative placements.

Source: https://www.americanbar.org/content/dam/aba/publications/center_on_children_and_the_law/resourcecenter/california_nov05.authcheckdam.pdf

Court Appointed Special Advocate (CASA)

CASA volunteers are appointed by judges to advocate for the best interests of abused and neglected children in court and other settings. The primary responsibilities of a CASA volunteer are to

- Gather information: Review documents and records; interview the children, family members, and professionals in their lives.
- Document findings: Provide written reports at court hearings.
- Appear in court: Advocate for the child's best interests and provide testimony when necessary.
- Explain what is going on: Help the child understand the court proceedings.
- Seek cooperative solutions: Among individuals and organizations involved in the children's lives.
- Recommend services: Ensure that the children and their family are receiving appropriate services and advocate for those that are not immediately available. Bring concerns about the child's health, education, mental health, etc. to the appropriate professionals.
- Monitor case plans and court orders: Check to see that plans are being followed and mandated review hearings are being held.
- Keep the court informed: Update the court on developments with agencies and family members. Ensure that appropriate motions are filed on behalf of the child so the court knows about any changes in the child's situation.

Adapted from: http://www.casaforchildren.org/site/c.mtJSJ7MPIsE/b.6350721/k.112A/What_Does_It_Mean_To_Be_a_CASA_Volunteer.htm

Most California counties have a local CASA program. *Source: http://www.californiacasa.org/who-we-are/casa-history/*

Dependent of the Court

If the juvenile court finds at the jurisdiction hearing that the child was abused or neglected, the court may decide to make the child a dependent of the court. The court becomes responsible for the care and custody of the dependent child.

Adapted from: http://www.families4children.com/adopt_jcdp.cfm

Educational Rights

Foster youth under age 18 must have an education rights holder who is required to make education decisions that are in the youth's best interest. Foster youth who are 18 or older have the right to make their own decisions about their education. The person who holds education rights may be the parent or legal guardian, the substitute caregiver, or another person chosen by the court. The social worker, attorney, or group home or school staff members may not be the education rights holder.

Adapted from: https://www.cde.ca.gov/ls/pf/fy/fosteryouthedrights.asp

Emancipation

Emancipation is a legal process that frees a child who is between the ages of 14 and 18 from the custody and control of their parents or guardian. In California, there are three ways to get emancipated. First, a minor can obtain a declaration of emancipation (a court order) from a judge. Second, a minor can get legally married with consent of your parents and permission from a court. Third, a minor can join the U.S. military on active duty.

Adapted from: http://www.courts.ca.gov/documents/emancipation_manual.pdf

Family Finding

Family finding aims to help children, adolescents, and youth in foster care reestablish family connections before they age out of foster care. Family finding programs work to identify family members and other adults close to foster care children, increase the children's sense of family connectedness, and involve these adults in developing and carrying out a plan for emotional and legal permanency.

Adapted from: https://www.childtrends.org/programs/family-finding/

Fictive Kin

Fictive kin is a person not related to a child by blood or marriage but who has a significant and positive relationship with a child; this person may be a godparent, neighbor, or family friend.

Adapted from: http://www.ncsl.org/research/human-services/the-child-welfare-placement-continuum-what-s-best-for-children.aspx

In California, fictive kin are typically referred to as non-related extended family member (NREFM). A "non-related extended family member" (NREFM) is defined as an adult caregiver who has an established familial relationship with a relative of the child or a familial or mentoring relationship with the child. The county welfare department verifies the existence of a relationship through interviews with the parent and child or with one or more third parties. The parties may include relatives of the child, teachers, medical professionals, clergy, neighbors, and family friends.

Adapted from: http://www.cdss.ca.gov/inforesources/Foster-Care/Kinship-Care

Foster Care Payments

Kinship care providers, foster families, FFAs, and group homes may receive payments to compensate for the costs of caring for children placed in out-of-home care.

In California, a relative or NREFM who is caring for a dependent child may be eligible to receive a monthly foster care maintenance payment whether the child is federally eligible or ineligible. These payments are used to offset the costs of providing the child with food, clothing, extracurricular activities, and other necessities.

Adapted from: http://www.cdss.ca.gov/inforesources/Foster-Care/Kinship-Care

As of January 1, 2015, California implemented a new county-optional program titled the Approved Relative Caregiver Funding Option Program that provides funding for participating counties to make per-child, per-month payments to approved relative caregivers on behalf of non-federally eligible children in an amount equal to the basic foster care rate paid to Aid to Families with Dependent Children-Foster Care (AFDC-FC) providers.

Adapted from: http://www.cdss.ca.gov/inforesources/Foster-Care/
Approved-Relative-Care

Kinship Guardianship Assistance Payment (Kin-GAP)

Kin-GAP is a cash aid program that supports eligible relative caregivers in California who are unable or unwilling to adopt but instead become legal guardians as the permanency option for exiting the child welfare system. Kin-GAP was established effective January 1, 2000, for children whose California Juvenile Court dependency is terminated in favor of guardianship with the relative caregiver. Kin-GAP provides both cash aid and Medi-Cal benefits to eligible children. Kin-GAP payments are income to the child, not to the caregiver.

Adapted from: http://www.fosterfamilyhelp.ca.gov/PG3037.htm

Foster Family Agency

Nonprofit agencies licensed to recruit, certify, train, and support foster parents for hard-to-place children who would otherwise require group home care.

Adapted from: http://www.ppic.org/content/pubs/report/R_510CDR.pdf

Foster Home

Family residences in which foster parents provide 24-hour care for no more than six children (with the exception of sibling groups).

Source: http://www.ppic.org/content/pubs/report/R_510CDR.pdf

Group Home

Structured, residential facilities that have a treatment component for children and youth who have been placed in foster care.

Adapted from: http://www.ppic.org/content/pubs/report/R_510CDR.pdf

Group homes provide the most restrictive out-of-home placement option for children in foster care. They provide a placement option for children with significant emotional or behavioral problems who require more restrictive environments. The licensed group home is defined as a facility of any capacity which provides 24-hour non-medical care and supervision to children in a structured environment, with such services provided at least in part by staff employed by the licensee. Group homes run the gamut from large institutional type environments which provide an intense therapeutic setting, often called "residential treatment centers," to small home environments which incorporate a "house parent" model. As a result, group home placements provide various levels of structure, supervision, and services. There are 14 levels of care in California, with Level 14 providing the most intensive services for youth with the highest level of need.

Adapted from: http://www.cdss.ca.gov/inforesources/Foster-Care/Group-Homes

Home Study

The process of approving applicants for foster parent licensure consists of assessments or home studies of the applicant, the applicant's family, and the applicant's home environment to determine whether the home would be safe and appropriate for children in foster care. Onsite home visits are conducted to assess the suitability of the home to accommodate the needs of all family members, including the foster children. The condition of the home is evaluated to determine whether it is clean, safe, comfortable, and in conformance with agency regulations. The agency also may require an inspection by the state health department or a fire and safety inspection by the fire marshal. In addition, the social worker will conduct interviews with the applicants and all family members to assess their suitability to provide appropriate care for children in foster care. Personal references are contacted for further information. To ensure that the foster parents are healthy enough to provide appropriate care, the social worker may require the results of recent health examinations. Checks of criminal records and child abuse and neglect records also are included in the study.

Adapted from: https://www.childwelfare.gov/pubPDFs/homestudyreqs.pdf

Independent Living Skills

The Independent Living Program provides training, services, and benefits to assist current and former foster youth in achieving self-sufficiency prior to, and after leaving, the foster care system. In California, each county has the flexibility to design services to meet a wide range of individual needs and circumstances and to coordinate services with other federal and state agencies engaged in similar activities. Youth are eligible for ILP services from age 16 to the day before their 21st birthday.

Source: http://www.cdss.ca.gov/inforesources/Foster-Care/Independent-Living-Program

Indian Child Welfare Act (ICWA)

Enacted in 1978, ICWA established federal requirements that apply to state child custody proceedings involving an Indian child who is a member of or eligible for membership in a federally recognized tribe. It requires caseworkers to make several considerations when handling an ICWA case, including providing active efforts to the family, identifying a placement that fits under the ICWA preference provisions, notifying the child's tribe and the child's parents of the child custody proceeding, and working actively to involve the child's tribe and the child's parents in the proceedings.

Adapted from: https://www.nicwa.org/about-icwa/

Individualized Education Plan (IEP)

A plan or program that is developed to ensure that a child who has a disability identified under the law and is attending an elementary or secondary educational institution receives specialized instruction and related services.

Source: https://www.washington.edu/doit/what-difference-between-iep-and-504-plan

Informal Family Maintenance

If the investigation finds that the parents do not pose an immediate and high risk of maltreating their child or there is inconclusive evidence to substantiate abuse, the emergency response (ER) social worker can decide to leave the child at home and may offer caregivers up to 30 days of ER services or up to 6 months of voluntary family maintenance services. Thirty-day ER services (also called "pre-placement prevention activities") can be provided to families when there is a problem that does not require removal of the child and when the social worker believes that the problem can be ameliorated within 30 days. Services can include emergency shelter care, temporary in-home caregivers, therapeutic day services, parenting training, substance abuse testing, transportation, and respite. Each county decides to what extent it wants to utilize this intervention. Voluntary family maintenance, also known as "informal supervision" (or informal family maintenance) means that if the family does not improve within the six-month period, a juvenile dependency court petition can be filed on the original allegations. Family maintenance services can include counseling, parent training, substance abuse treatment, respite care, or other services that meet identified needs. The family agrees to accept these services on a voluntary basis without court intervention. At the end of the 30-day or 6-month period, the case is either closed or referred to juvenile dependency court if there is a new report of suspected child abuse or the social worker determines that voluntary services have been unsuccessful.

Adapted from: http://www.dhcs.ca.gov/formsandpubs/publications/Documents/CMS/ ChildWelfarePrimer.pdf

Interviewing Center

A comfortable, private, child-focused setting where forensic interviews of children and youth are conducted. The interviews are conducted by a competently trained, neutral professional using methods that are developmentally sensitive and legally sound to gather factual information regarding allegations of abuse.

Adapted from: https://www.ojjdp.gov/pubs/248749.pdf

Investigation

After receiving a report, child welfare agencies conduct an initial assessment or investigation to determine 1) if child maltreatment occurred; 2) if the child's immediate safety is a concern and, if it is, the interventions that will ensure the child's protection while keeping the child within the family or with family members if at all possible; 3) if there is a risk of future maltreatment and the level of that risk; 4) if continuing agency services are needed to address any effects of child maltreatment and to reduce the risk of future maltreatment.

Adapted from: https://www.childwelfare.gov/pubPDFs/cps.pdf

Involuntary Psychiatric Hold

The conditions under which a child who is experiencing a psychiatric crisis may be involuntarily hospitalized are governed by California state law. The child must, as a result of a mental disorder, be "gravely disabled" or pose a danger to him/herself or others (e.g., unable to use the elements of life which are essential to health, safety, and development, including food, clothing, and shelter, even though provided to the minor by others). Only peace officers; members of the attending staff of an evaluation facility designated by the county, such as a Department of Mental Health clinic or a specified psychiatric hospital; or designated members of a mobile crisis team are authorized to take a child into custody and place him or her in a psychiatric hospital. The child may be held in the facility for a period of up to 72 hours, excluding holidays and weekends.

Adapted from: http://policy.dcfs.lacounty.gov/Content/Attachments/060050520_att1.pdf

Juvenile Dependency Court

The court's authority for dependency cases is found within the California Welfare and Institutions Code. The court's role is to ensure that the rights of children and their families are protected in accordance with the law designed to protect abused and neglected children. During hearings, the court may consider information about the alleged abuse or neglect, the well-being of the children, police and social worker reports, medical and psychiatric reports, family history, placement options, and oral arguments from attorneys. Testimony may be heard from people such as social worker(s), police officers, parents, family members, doctors, teachers, witnesses, and in some cases, the child(ren). County child welfare agencies are accountable to the juvenile courts as they propose outcomes for initial case disposition hearings and review hearings.

Adapted from: https://www.advokids.org/legal-tools/juvenile-court-process/

Juvenile Court—Consolidated

When juveniles are simultaneously involved in the child welfare and juvenile justice systems (dual status minors), hearings for juvenile delinquency related matters may be heard in a consolidated juvenile court process. Under Assembly Bill 129, "the probation department and the child welfare services department, in consultation with the presiding judge of the juvenile court, in any county may create a jointly written protocol to allow the county probation department and the child welfare services department to jointly assess and produce a recommendation that the child be designated as a dual status child, allowing the child to be simultaneously a dependent child and a ward of the court."

Adapted from: http://www.courts.ca.gov/documents/AB129bill-chaptered.pdf

Juvenile Hall

California divides control over juvenile confinement facilities between state and county governments. The state agency primarily responsible for incarcerating young offenders—the California Youth Authority—operates large institutions where (generally the most serious) offenders are committed by county juvenile courts for long-term placement. The state has little direct role in the operation of detention facilities (known as juvenile halls) or local commitment facilities (i.e., probation camps and ranches) that are operated and funded by county governments, although it exercises some regulatory control over them through the California Board of Corrections.

Source: https://www.urban.org/sites/default/files/publication/60466/410529-Youth-Corrections-in-California.PDF

Legal Guardianship

Legal guardianship involves a court order that says someone who is not the child's parent is in charge of taking care of the child. Legal guardians have many of the same rights and responsibilities as parents.

Guardianship is most frequently used by relative caregivers who wish to provide a permanent home for the child and maintain relationships with extended family members. Unlike adoption requirements, caregivers can assume legal guardianship of a child in out-of-home care without termination of parental rights.

Source: http://www.fosterfamilyhelp.ca.gov/PG3015.htm

Licensed County Foster Care Provider

See State Licensing Board

Linkages

The California Linkages project is a statewide program that promotes collaboration between California's county-administered child welfare services and CalWORKs, the state's program for administering Temporary Assistance for Needy Families (TANF). The goal of Linkages is to decrease child maltreatment and improve outcomes for children and families by providing necessary services and supports through increased collaboration.

Adapted from: https://www.childwelfare.gov/topics/management/funding/funding-sources/federal-funding/cb-funding/cbreports/tanfcw/linkages/#tab=summary

LiveScan

Background checks for caregivers require fingerprinting in California; LiveScan refers to the electronic fingerprinting technology that is used.

Adapted from: http://www.cdss.ca.gov/inforesources/Community-Care/
Caregiver-Background-Check/LiveScan

Medi-Cal

The California Medical Assistance Program (Medi-Cal or MediCal) is California's Medicaid program serving low-income individuals, including families, seniors, persons with disabilities, children in foster care and former foster youth up to age 26, pregnant women, and childless adults with incomes below 138% of federal poverty level. Benefits include ambulatory patient services, emergency services, hospitalization, maternity and newborn care, mental health and substance use disorder treatment, dental, vision, and long-term care and supports.

Source: https://en.wikipedia.org/wiki/Medi-Cal

Non-Related Extended Family Member (NREFM)

See Fictive Kin

Parenting Class

As a core prevention service, parent education can be defined as any training, program, or other intervention that helps parents acquire skills to improve their parenting of and communication with their children in order to reduce the risk of child maltreatment and/or reduce children's disruptive behaviors. Parent education may be delivered individually or in a group in the home, classroom, or other setting; it may be face-to-face or online; and it may include direct instruction, discussion, videos, modeling, or other formats.

Adapted from: https://www.childwelfare.gov/pubPDFs/parented.pdf

Paternity

Adjudicated Father

An adjudicated father is a man that has an existing judicial determination that a parent-child relationship exists. Similar to a biological father, an adjudicated father may be granted family reunification services (but is not necessarily entitled to them) if he can persuade the court that reunification services will be in the best interests of the child.

Source: https://www.advokids.org/legal-tools/paternity-parentage/

Alleged Father

An alleged father is a man who may be the father of the child, but whose biological paternity has not been established or who has not achieved presumed father status. Alleged fathers have the right to receive notice of the dependency case and to appear before the court and assert an interest in the child by filing required forms.

An alleged father is not a party to the case until he has appeared before the court and does not have a right to custody.

Adapted from: https://www.advokids.org/legal-tools/paternity-parentage/

Biological Father

A biological father is a father who is genetically the father of the child but who has failed to take any steps to become a presumed father. If biological fathers appear promptly after notice of the dependency case, then they have the right to develop a relationship with the child. A biological father may be granted family reunification services (but is not necessarily entitled to them) if he can persuade the court that reunification services will be in the best interests of the child.

Source: https://www.advokids.org/legal-tools/paternity-parentage/

Presumed Father

Refers to an individual whom the law presumes, until shown otherwise, to be the legal father of a child and who has the rights and responsibilities of a father, even if not a biological father. Presumed fathers are entitled to family reunification services if they request placement or custody of the child.

Source: https://www.advokids.org/legal-tools/paternity-parentage/

Petition

Juvenile dependency cases begin when a petition is filed by the child welfare agency under Welfare and Institutions Code (WIC) Section 300. This petition alleges that there is actual or immediate danger to a child. If the safety of the child cannot be assured at home, the child can be removed from the parents' custody and placed in protective custody.

Adapted from: http://www.lacourt.org/division/juvenile/JV0011.aspx

Placement Level of Care Level 14

See Group Homes

Protective Custody

A protective custody hold is when a child is removed from the custody of his or her parents by law enforcement personnel or a child welfare services social worker and placed with a relative, a non-related extended family member (NREFM), or in a foster home because there is reasonable cause to believe the child is described by Welfare and Institutions Code (WIC) Section 300 and there are no reasonable means to protect the child without removal.

Adapted from: https://www.dhhs.saccounty.net/CPS/Documents/Emergency-Response/
Protective%20Custody%20Information%20Sheet.pdf

Referral

Child welfare agencies are responsible for receiving and evaluating referrals or reports of suspected child abuse and neglect made by members of the community, law enforcement personnel, or education or medical professionals.

Adapted from: https://www.childwelfare.gov/pubPDFs/cps.pdf

Regional Center

Regional Centers are nonprofit private organizations that contract with the California Department of Developmental Services to provide or coordinate services and supports for individuals with developmental disabilities. They have offices throughout California to provide a local resource to help find and access the services available to individuals and their families.

Source: https://www.dds.ca.gov/RC/

Selection and Termination Hearing

See Court Hearings

Seven-Day Notice

The foster parent(s) shall be given at least seven calendar days' advance written notice of intent to remove a child and of the right to request a grievance review. The exceptions to the seven-day notice will be 1) the child is in immediate danger, 2) a signed waiver of notice has been obtained from the foster parent(s), 3) a court has ordered the child's removal, 4) adverse licensing or approval actions have occurred that prohibit the foster parent(s) from continuing to provide services, 5) removal of a voluntarily placed child is made or requested by the child's parent(s)/guardians, or 6) The child is removed from an emergency placement.

Source: https://33lgab6r1t73tftdv36ttnxi-wpengine.netdna-ssl.com/wp-content/uploads/pdf/DSS-Manual-Abridged.pdf#page=7

Foster parents may submit a seven-day notice: There are times when a foster family and a foster child are not a good "fit" despite everyone's best efforts. In order to accomplish a change in placement, you will need to give the social worker a seven-day notice that you want the child removed, unless there are special circumstances that would require immediate removal. It is important that you actively participate in the transition plan.

Source: http://www.fosterfamilyhelp.ca.gov/PG3062.htm#A12

SSI (Supplemental Security Income)

Supplemental Security Income (SSI) is a federal income supplement program funded by general tax revenues (not Social Security taxes). It is designed to help aged, blind, and disabled people who have little or no income and provides cash to meet basic needs for food, clothing, and shelter.

Adapted from: https://www.ssa.gov/ssi/

State Disability Insurance Benefits

Disability insurance is a component of the State Disability Insurance (SDI) program, established in 1946, to provide partial wage replacement benefits to eligible California workers who are unable to work due to a non-work-related illness, injury, or pregnancy.

Source: http://www.edd.ca.gov/Disability/About_DI.htm

State Licensing Board

The California Department of Social Services operates the Children's Residential Licensing Program which licenses and monitors adoption agencies, foster family agencies, certified family homes, group homes, foster family homes, crisis nurseries, runaway youth shelters, small family homes, and transitional housing placement programs in an effort to ensure that they provide a safe and healthy environment for children who are in residential care.

Adapted from: http://www.cdss.ca.gov/inforesources/Childrens-Residential/
How-to-Become-Licensed

Stipulation

In juvenile dependency proceedings, parents may stipulate to the jurisdiction of the dependency court (i.e., formally acknowledge as true the allegations being made by the child welfare agency).

Adapted from: http://www.courts.ca.gov/documents/CIPReassessmentRpt.pdf

Student Study Team (SST)

An SST is a function of regular education, not special education, and is governed by school district policy rather than federal or state law. It is not mandatory to have an SST prior to an IEP or referral for special education assessment. Students struggling in school may be referred to an SST. An SST can be the first step towards determining whether a student needs special education services.

Source: http://www.publiccounsel.org/tools/publications/files/Ed-Law-Factsheets-
FINAL-DRAFT-12-14-10.pdf

Substantiate/Evaluate Out

At the end of an investigation, CWS caseworkers typically make one of two findings: unsubstantiated (unfounded) or substantiated (founded). These terms vary from state to state. Typically, a finding of unsubstantiated means there is insufficient evidence for the worker to conclude that a child was abused or neglected, or what happened does not meet the legal definition of child abuse or neglect. A finding of substantiated typically means that an incident of child abuse or neglect, as defined by state law, is believed to have occurred. Some states have additional categories, such as "unable to determine," that suggest there was not enough evidence to either confirm or refute that abuse or neglect occurred.

Adapted from: https://www.childwelfare.gov/pubPDFs/cpswork.pdf

California

When a CWS agency receives a report of suspected child abuse or neglect (which is also called a "referral"), county CWS social workers investigate the report to determine if the alleged child maltreatment is "substantiated" as defined in state law. Substantiated reports require further action by the CWS agency and can result in either the agency providing supportive services to the child and family or, if there is imminent risk to the child's safety, the CWS agency removing the child from the home. In addition to substantiated reports, state law and CWS practice also define various types of unsubstantiated reports—"inconclusive," "unfounded," and "evaluated out" reports. The following are descriptions of the possible case dispositions following a report of child maltreatment:

- Evaluated Out—based upon the information in the initial referral, the CWS agency determined that no child maltreatment (as defined in statute) has occurred, and no further investigation is conducted. (This category of case disposition is not defined in statute, but is used in practice.)
- Unfounded—the investigator determined that the referral was false, improbable, or otherwise did not meet the statutory definition of child maltreatment.
- Inconclusive—the investigator did not determine that the alleged child maltreatment was unfounded, but there was insufficient evidence to substantiate the report.
- Substantiated—the investigator determined, based upon available evidence, that child maltreatment more likely than not occurred.

Adapted from: http://www.lao.ca.gov/reports/2013/ssrv/child-neglect/child-neglect-080813.pdf

Supplemental Petition

California Welfare and Institutions Code section 387 provides that

a. An order changing or modifying a previous order by removing a child from the physical custody of a parent, guardian, relative, or friend and directing placement in a foster home, or commitment to a private or county institution, shall be made only after noticed hearing upon a supplemental petition.

b. The supplemental petition shall be filed by the social worker in the original matter and shall contain a concise statement of facts sufficient to support the conclusion that the previous disposition has not been effective in the rehabilitation or protection of the child or, in the case of a placement with a relative, sufficient to show that the placement is not appropriate in view of the criteria in Section 361.3.

Source: http://leginfo.legislature.ca.gov/faces/codes_displaySection.xhtml?lawCode=WIC&sectionNum=387

Team Decision Making (TDM)

TDM focuses on placement issues for children involved or potentially involved in foster care. This team meeting involves, in addition to caseworkers and their supervisors, birth families, community members, resource families, and service providers in all placement decisions regarding foster children. These meetings must occur prior to the decision or court hearing.

Adapted from: https://www.advokids.org/childhood-mental-health/
team-decision-making-tdm/

Currently, 25 of the 58 California counties participate in the Family to Family Initiative and approximately 88% of the 78,960 children in California child welfare supervised foster care are living in a Family to Family county.

Source: http://www.f2f.ca.gov/aboutus.htm

Strategies utilized include:

- Recruiting, developing, and supporting resource families.
- Building community partnerships.
- Making decisions as a team.
- Evaluating results.

Adapted from: http://www.f2f.ca.gov/res/F2FOurwork.pdf

THC

THC, or delta-9-tetrahydrocannabinol, is the main psychoactive (mind-altering) chemical in marijuana, responsible for most of the intoxicating effects that people seek.

Adapted from: https://www.drugabuse.gov/publications/research-reports/marijuana/
what-marijuana

Trafficker

Under U.S. law, human trafficking is defined as "sex trafficking in which a commercial sex act is induced by force, fraud, or coercion, or in which the person induced to perform such act has not attained 18 years of age," or "the recruitment, harboring, transportation, provision, or obtaining of a person for labor or services through the use of force, fraud, or coercion for the purpose of subjection to involuntary servitude, peonage, debt bondage, or slavery." Human trafficking can involve transnational recruitment of victims who are then transported across borders into another country where they are exploited for labor and/or sex. Human trafficking can also occur domestically, where little or no transportation is involved in recruitment and exploitation of victims.

Adapted from: https://www.humanrightsfirst.org/resource/who-are-human-traffickers

Transitional Housing Program

Transitional housing refers to a supportive—yet temporary—type of accommodation that is meant to bridge the gap from homelessness to permanent housing by offering structure, supervision, support (for addictions and mental health, for instance), life skills, and in some cases, education and training.

Source: http://homelesshub.ca/solutions/housing-accommodation-and-supports/
transitional-housing

Victim of Crime Referral

The California Department of Corrections and Rehabilitation's Office of Victim and Survivor Rights and Services (OVSRS) maintains a victim services program that is responsible for providing information, notification, restitution, outreach, training, referral, and support services to crime victims and their next of kin.

Adapted from: https://www.cdcr.ca.gov/Victim_Services/

Visitation Center/Supervised Visitation

Supervised family visitation centers (FVC) provide an alternative setting where children can visit with their parents in a safe environment and where objective observers can monitor visits. FVC supervisors often are trained observers who can serve as a rich source of information about parent-child interaction in times when permanency decisions are required more rapidly.

Adapted from: https://onlinelibrary.wiley.com/doi/full/10.1111/j.0022-2445.2004.0005.x

Welfare and Institutions Code (WIC) Section 300

WIC 300 sets forth the criteria used by California juvenile dependency courts to determine whether a child should be adjudged a dependent of the court.

Adapted from: http://leginfo.legislature.ca.gov/faces/codes_displaySection.
xhtml?lawCode=WIC&sectionNum=300.

Wraparound Services

Wraparound is a strengths-based planning process that occurs in a team setting to engage with children, youth, and their families in order to help families achieve positive goals and improve well-being. Wraparound is also a team-driven process. The team works directly with the family as they identify their own needs and strengths, developing an individualized service plan that describes specific strategies for meeting the needs identified by the family, with strategies that reflect the child and family's culture and preferences.

Adapted from: http://www.cdss.ca.gov/inforesources/Foster-Care/
Family-Centered-Services

Glossary References

1. **504 Supportive Services**
   U.S. Department of Health And Human Services Office for Civil Rights Administration for Children and Families & U.S. Department of Justice Civil Rights Division Disability Rights Section. (2015). *Protecting the rights of parents and prospective parents with disabilities: Technical assistance for state and local child welfare agencies and courts under Title II of the Americans with Disabilities Act and Section 504 of the Rehabilitation Act.* Retrieved from https://www.ada.gov/doj_hhs_ta/child_welfare_ta.html
   Alameda Unified School District. (n.d.). *Section 504 Plans.* Retrieved from https://www.alameda.k12.ca.us/studentservices#Section504

2. **Seven-Day Notice**
   a. State of California Health and Human Services Agency Department of Social Services. (2003). *Manual and policies procedures child welfare services.* Retrieved from https://33lgab6r1t73tftdv36ttnxi-wpengine.netdna-ssl.com/wp-content/uploads/pdf/DSS-Manual-Abridged.pdf#page=7
   b. California Department of Social Services. (2007). Caregiver frequently asked questions (FAQs). Retrieved from http://www.fosterfamilyhelp.ca.gov/PG3062.htm#A12

3. **Alternate/Other Permanent Planning Living Arrangement**
   Child Welfare Information Gateway. (n.d.). *OPPLA/APPLA.* Retrieved from https://www.childwelfare.gov/topics/outofhome/foster-care/oppla-appla/

4. **Alternative Response/Differential Response**
   California Department of Social Services. (2018). *Differential response.* Retrieved from http://www.cdss.ca.gov/inforesources/Child-Welfare-Protection/Differential-Response

5. **AWOL**
   San Diego State University School of Social Work Academy for Professional Excellence. (2018). *PCWTA curriculum: Understanding and managing AWOL behaviors in out-of-home placement.* Retrieved from https://theacademy.sdsu.edu/pcwtacurriculum/understanding-and-managing-awol-behaviors-in-out-of-home-placement/

6. **Background Check**
   Child Welfare Information Gateway. (2016). *Background checks for prospective foster, adoptive, and kinship caregivers.* Washington, DC: U.S. Department of Health and Human Services, Children's Bureau. Retrieved from https://www.childwelfare.gov/pubPDFs/background.pdf#page=5&view=Summaries%20of%20State%20laws

7. **Behavioral/Educational Surrogate**
   California Foster Youth Education Task Force. (2017). *California foster care education law fact sheets* [Fact Sheet]. Retrieved from http://www.cfyetf.org/publications_19_421458854.pdf

8. **Bypass**
   Schwarz, Shawna Hon. (2012). *Bypass-at-a-glance* (v.1.0). Retrieved from http://cadependencyonlineguide.info/view/articles/11986.pdf

9. **CalWORKs**
   California Department of Social Services. (2018). *California Work Opportunity and Responsibility to Kids (CalWORKs).* Retrieved from http://www.cdss.ca.gov/CalWORKs

10. **Caregiver/Relative Approval and Exemptions**
    advokids. (2017). Resource family approval. Retrieved from https://www.advokids.org/resource-family-approval-rfa-program/

11. **Case Plan**
    Child Welfare Information Gateway. (2014). *Case planning for families involved with child welfare agencies.* Washington, DC: U.S. Department of Health and Human Services, Children's Bureau. Retrieved from https://www.childwelfare.gov/pubPDFs/caseplanning.pdf

12. **Commercially Sexually Exploited Child (CSEC)**
    California Child Welfare Council. (n.d.). *Prevalence of commercially sexually exploited children* [Fact Sheet]. Retrieved from http://www.chhs.ca.gov/Child%20Welfare/CSEC%20Fact%20Sheet%20-%201.pdf

13. **Concurrent Plan/Concurrent Planning**
    Child Welfare Information Gateway. (n.d.). *Concurrent planning.* Retrieved from https://www.childwelfare.gov/topics/permanency/planning/concurrent/

14. **Court Hearings**
    a. The Judicial Branch of California. (2018). *Juvenile dependency flow chart* [Flow Chart]. Retrieved from http://www.courts.ca.gov/documents/Dependency_Flow_chart.pdf

b. Superior Court of California County of Alameda. (n.d.). *What kinds of legal hearings are held in juvenile dependency court?* Retrieved from http://www.alameda.courts.ca.gov/Pages.aspx/ Dependency-Legal-Hearings

c. **366.26 Selection and Implementation Hearing**
Administrative Office of the Courts Center for Families, Children and the Courts. (2005). *California Juvenile Dependency Court Improvement Program Reassessment.* Retrieved from http://www.courts.ca.gov/ documents/CIPReassessmentRpt.pdf

d. **Contested Hearing**
California Courts The Judicial Branch of California. (2018). *2018 California rules of court.* Retrieved from http://www.courts.ca.gov/cms/rules/ index.cfm?title=five&linkid=rule5_684

e. **Continuance/Continued Hearing**
Social Services Agency Department of Family and Children Services. (2007). *DFCS online policies & procedures* [Handbook]. Retrieved from https://www.sccgov.org/ssa/opp2/08_juvenilecourt/8-4.html
WIC 352 (a)
FindLaw For Legal Professionals. (2018). *California Code, Welfare and Institution Code—WIC § 352.* Retrieved from https://codes.findlaw.com/ ca/welfare-and-institutions-code/wic-sect-352.html

f. **Interim Review Hearing**
Administrative Office of the Courts Center for Families, Children and the Courts. (2005). *California Juvenile Dependency Court Improvement Program Reassessment.* Retrieved from https://www.americanbar.org/ content/dam/aba/publications/center_on_children_and_the_law/ resourcecenter/california_nov05.authcheckdam.pdf

15. **County Assessment Center**
a. San Bernadino County Children and Family Services. (2016). *2016 annual report.* Retrieved from http://hs.sbcounty.gov/cfs/Documents/ Annual%20report.pdf

b. San Diego Health and Human Services Agency Child Welfare Services. (2011). California Outcomes and Accountability System Child and Family Services Review 2011 County Self Assessment Report County of San Diego. Retrieved from https://www.sandiegocounty.gov/content/dam/sdc/ hhsa/programs/cs/documents/San_Diego_2011_CSA_Report.pdf

16. **Court Appointed Special Advocate (CASA)**
a. Court Appointed Special Advocates for Children. (2017). *What does it mean to be a CASA volunteer?* Retrieved from http://www. casaforchildren.org/site/c.mtJSJ7MPIsE/b.6350721/k.112A/What_Does_ It_Mean_To_Be_a_CASA_Volunteer.htm

b. California Court Appointed Special Advocates for Children. (2018). *CASA history*. Retrieved from http://www.californiacasa.org/who-we-are/casa-history/

17. Dependent of the Court

Families for Children. (2013). *Description of juvenile court dependency process*. Retrieved from
http://www.families4children.com/adopt_jcdp.cfm

18. Educational Rights

California Department of Education. (2017). *Foster youth education rights*. Retrieved from
https://www.cde.ca.gov/ls/pf/fy/fosteryouthedrights.asp

19. Emancipation

Legal Services for Children Inc. (2012). *Legal services for children emancipation manual*. Retrieved from
http://www.courts.ca.gov/documents/emancipation_manual.pdf

20. Family Finding

Child Trends. (2017). *Family finding*. Retrieved from
https://www.childtrends.org/programs/family-finding/

21. Fictive Kin

a. National Conference of State Legislatures. (2016). *The child welfare placement continuum: What's best for children?* Retrieved from http://www.ncsl.org/research/human-services/the-child-welfare-placement-continuum-what-s-best-for-children.aspx

b. California Department of Social Services. (2018). *Kinship care*. Retrieved from http://www.cdss.ca.gov/inforesources/Foster-Care/Kinship-Care

22. Foster Care Payments

a. California Department of Social Services. (2018). *Kinship care*. Retrieved from http://www.cdss.ca.gov/inforesources/Foster-Care/Kinship-Care

b. California Department of Social Services. (2018). *Approved Relative Caregiver (ARC) Funding Option Program*. Retrieved from http://www.cdss.ca.gov/inforesources/Foster-Care/Approved-Relative-Care

c. Kinship Guardianship Assistance Payment (Kin-GAP)
California Department of Social Services. (2007). *Kinship Guardianship Assistance Payment (Kin-GAP)*. Retrieved from http://www.fosterfamilyhelp.ca.gov/PG3037.htm

23. Foster Family Agency

Danielson, C., & Lee, H. (2010). *Foster care in California: Achievements and challenges*. Retrieved from Public Policy Institute of California
http://www.ppic.org/content/pubs/report/R_510CDR.pdf

24. **Foster Home**
    Danielson, C., & Lee, H. (2010). *Foster care in California: Achievements and challenges.* Retrieved from Public Policy Institute of California
    http://www.ppic.org/content/pubs/report/R_510CDR.pdf

25. **Group Home**
    a. Danielson, C., & Lee, H. (2010). *Foster care in California: Achievements and challenges.* Retrieved from Public Policy Institute of California
        http://www.ppic.org/content/pubs/report/R_510CDR.pdf
    b. California Department of Social Services. (2018). *Group homes.* Retrieved from http://www.cdss.ca.gov/inforesources/Foster-Care/Group-Homes

26. **Home Study**
    Child Welfare Information Gateway. (n.d.). *Home study requirements for prospective foster parents.* Retrieved from
    https://www.childwelfare.gov/pubPDFs/homestudyreqs.pdf

27. **Indian Child Welfare Act (ICWA)**
    National Indian Child Welfare Association. (2018). *About ICWA.*
    Retrieved from
    https://www.nicwa.org/about-icwa/

28. **Individualized Education Plan (IEP)**
    DO-IT, University of Washington. (2017). *What is the difference between an IEP and a 504 Plan?* Retrieved from
    https://www.washington.edu/doit/what-difference-between-iep-and-504-plan

29. **Independent Living Skills**
    California Department of Social Services. (2018). *Independent Living Program (ILP).* Retrieved from
    http://www.cdss.ca.gov/inforesources/Foster-Care/Independent-Living-Program

30. **Informal Family Maintenance**
    Reed, D. F., & Karpilow, K, (2002). *Understanding the child welfare system in California: A primer for service providers and policymakers.* Retrieved from
    California Center for Research on Women and Families
    http://www.dhcs.ca.gov/formsandpubs/publications/Documents/CMS/ChildWelfarePrimer.pdf

31. **Interviewing Center**
    Newlin, C., Cordisco Steele, L., Chamberlin, A., Anderson, J., Kenniston, J., Russell, A., ... Vaughan-Eden, V. (2015). *Child forensic interviewing: Best practices* [Bulletin]. Retrieved from U.S. Department of Justice, Office of Justice Programs, Office of Juvenile Justice and Delinquency Prevention
    https://www.ojjdp.gov/pubs/248749.pdf

32. Investigation

DePanfilis, D., & Salus, M. K. (2003). *Child protective services: A guide for caseworkers* [Manual]. Retrieved from U.S. Department of Health and Human Services Administration for Children and Families, Administration on Children, Youth and Families, Children's Bureau, Office on Child Abuse and Neglect

https://www.childwelfare.gov/pubPDFs/cps.pdf

33. Involuntary Psychiatric Hold

County of Los Angeles Department of Child and Family Services. (n.d.). *Involuntary psychiatric hospitalization when a child is in crisis* [Child Welfare Policy Manual]. Retrieved from

http://policy.dcfs.lacounty.gov/Content/Attachments/060050520_att1.pdf

34. Juvenile Dependency Court

    a.   advokids. (2017). *Dependency court process*. Retrieved from https://www.advokids.org/legal-tools/juvenile-court-process/

    b.   Juvenile Court—Consolidated
California Courts The Judicial Branch of California. (2016). *Assembly Bill No. 129*. Retrieved from http://www.courts.ca.gov/documents/AB129bill-chaptered.pdf

35. Juvenile Hall

    a.   Steinhart, D., & Butts, J. A. (2002). *Youth corrections in California* [Research Report]. Retrieved from Urban Institute Justice Policy Center https://www.urban.org/sites/default/files/publication/60466/410529-Youth-Corrections-in-California.PDF

36. Legal Guardianship

California Department of Social Services. (2017). *Legal guardianship*. Retrieved from http://www.fosterfamilyhelp.ca.gov/PG3015.htm

    a.   **Licensed County Foster Care Provider**
(see State Licensing Board)

    b.   **Linkages**

        i.   Child Welfare Information Gateway. (2012). *The California Linkages Project*. Retrieved from https://www.childwelfare.gov/topics/management/funding/funding-sources/federal-funding/cb-funding/cbreports/tanfcw/linkages/#tab=summary

    c.   **LiveScan**

        i.   California Department of Social Services. (2018). *LiveScan application process and associated fees*. Retrieved from http://www.cdss.ca.gov/inforesources/Community-Care/Caregiver-Background-Check/LiveScan

d. **Medi-Cal**
   i. https://en.wikipedia.org/wiki/Medi-Cal
e. **Non-Related Extended Family Member (NREFM)**
   See Fictive Kin
f. **Parenting Class**
   i. Child Welfare Information Gateway. (2013). *Parent education to strengthen families and reduce the risk of maltreatment* [Issue Brief]. Retrieved from https://www.childwelfare.gov/pubPDFs/parented.pdf
g. **Paternity**
   i. Adjudicated Father
      advokids. (2017). *Paternity (or parentage).* Retrieved from https://www.advokids.org/legal-tools/paternity-parentage/
   ii. Alleged Father
      advokids. (2017). *Paternity (or parentage).* Retrieved from https://www.advokids.org/legal-tools/paternity-parentage/
   iii. Biological Father
      advokids. (2017). *Paternity (or parentage).* Retrieved from https://www.advokids.org/legal-tools/paternity-parentage/
   iv. Presumed Father
      advokids. (2017). *Paternity (or parentage).* Retrieved from https://www.advokids.org/legal-tools/paternity-parentage/
h. **Petition**
   i. The Superior Court of California County of Los Angeles. (2014). *What does juvenile dependency court do?* Retrieved from http://www.lacourt.org/division/juvenile/JV0011.aspx
i. **Placement Level of Care Level 14**
   See Group Homes
j. **Protective Custody**
   i. Sacramento County Department of Health and Human Services. (2013). *Sacramento County protective custody information sheet.* Retrieved from https://www.dhhs.saccounty.net/CPS/Documents/Emergency-Response/Protective%20Custody%20Information%20Sheet.pdf
k. **Referral**
   i. DePanfilis, D., & Salus, M. K. (2003). *Child protective services: A guide for caseworkers* [Manual]. Retrieved from U.S. Department of Health and Human Services Administration for Children and Families, Administration on Children, Youth and Families, Children's Bureau, Office on Child Abuse and Neglect https://www.childwelfare.gov/pubPDFs/cps.pdf

l. **Regional Center**
   i. State of California Department of Developmental Services. (2018). *Information about regional centers*. Retrieved from https://www.dds.ca.gov/RC/

m. **Selection and Termination Hearing**
   See Court Hearings/Terminating Parental Rights

n. **SSI (Supplemental Security Income)**
   i. Social Security Administration. (2018). *Supplemental Security Income home page—2018 edition*. Retrieved from https://www.ssa.gov/ssi/

o. **Student Study Team (SST)**
   i. California Foster Youth Education Task Force. (2010). *California foster care education law factsheets* (4th ed.). Retrieved from http://www.publiccounsel.org/tools/publications/files/Ed-Law-Factsheets-FINAL-DRAFT-12-14-10.pdf

p. **State Disability Insurance Benefits**
   i. State of California Employment Development Department. (2018). *About disability insurance (DI)*. Retrieved from http://www.edd.ca.gov/Disability/About_DI.htm

q. **State Licensing Board**
   i. California Department of Social Services. (2018). *How to become licensed or approved*. Retrieved from http://www.cdss.ca.gov/inforesources/Childrens-Residential/How-to-Become-Licensed

r. **Stipulation**
   Center for Families, Children and the Courts. (2005). *California Juvenile Dependency Court Improvement Program Reassessment*. Retrieved from http://www.courts.ca.gov/documents/CIPReassessmentRpt.pdf

s. **Substantiate/Evaluate Out**
   i. Child Welfare Information Gateway. (2013). *How the child welfare system works* [Fact Sheet]. Retrieved from https://www.childwelfare.gov/pubPDFs/cpswork.pdf
   ii. California
   Taylor, M. (2013). *Protecting children from abuse and neglect: Trends and issues* [Report]. Retrieved from California Legislative Analyst's Office http://www.lao.ca.gov/reports/2013/ssrv/child-neglect/child-neglect-080813.pdf

t. **Supplemental Petition**
   i. California Legislative Information. (2018). *Welfare and Institutions Code—WIC*. Retrieved from http://leginfo.legislature.ca.gov/faces/codes_displaySection.xhtml?lawCode=WIC&sectionNum=387

u. **Team Decision Making (TDM)**

   i. advokids. (2017). *Team Decision Making (TDM).* Retrieved from https://www.advokids.org/childhood-mental-health/team-decision-making-tdm/

   ii. Family to Family California. (2018). *About us.* Retrieved from http://www.f2f.ca.gov/aboutus.htm

   iii. Family to Family California. (n.d.). *Family to Family: Our work* [Fact Sheet]. Retrieved from http://www.f2f.ca.gov/res/F2FOurwork.pdf

v. **THC**

   i. National Institute on Drug Abuse. (2018). *Marijuana.* Retrieved from https://www.drugabuse.gov/publications/research-reports/marijuana/what-marijuana

w. **Trafficker**

   i. Human Rights First. (2014). *Who are human traffickers?* Retrieved from https://www.humanrightsfirst.org/resource/who-are-human-traffickers

x. **Transitional Housing Program**

   i. Homeless Hub 10 Years. (2017). *Transitional housing.* Retrieved from http://homelesshub.ca/solutions/housing-accommodation-and-supports/transitional-housing

y. **Victim of Crime Referral**

   i. California Department of Corrections and Rehabilitation. (2017). *Victim & survivor rights & services.* Retrieved from https://www.cdcr.ca.gov/Victim_Services/

z. **Visitation Center/Supervised Visitation**

   i. McWey, L. M., & Mullis, A. K. (2005). Improving the lives of children in foster care: The impact of supervised visitation. *Family Relations Interdisciplinary Journal of Applied Family Science, 3*(1), 293–300. Retrieved from https://onlinelibrary.wiley.com/doi/pdf/10.1111/j.0022-2445.2004.0005.x

aa. **Welfare and Institutions Code (WIC) Section 300**

   i. California Legislative Information. (2016). *Welfare and Institutions Code—WIC.* Retrieved from http://leginfo.legislature.ca.gov/faces/codes_displaySection.xhtml?lawCode=WIC&sectionNum=300

ab. **Wraparound Services**

   i. California Department of Social Services. (2018). *Family centered services: California Wraparound.* Retrieved from http://www.cdss.ca.gov/inforesources/Foster-Care/Family-Centered-Services

Index

About the Authors

Sarah Carnochan is the research director of the Mack Center on Nonprofit and Public Sector Management in the Human Services.

Lisa Molinar is the president of Shared Vision Consultants, Inc., a human services consulting agency that specializes in child welfare organizations.

Joanne Brown is a consultant with Shared Vision Consultants and a faculty member at the Center for Human Services at the University of California, Davis.

Lisa Botzler is a child welfare consultant with Shared Vision Consultants with many years of experience helping families and developing working relationships with community partners.

Karen Gunderson is a consultant with Shared Vision Consultants. She has more than 30 years of experience in child welfare, including eight years of direct service and 22 in policy and program development.

Colleen Henry is an assistant professor at the Silberman School of Social Work at Hunter College at the City University of New York.

Michael J. Austin is a professor of nonprofit management at the University of California, Berkeley, and the director of the Mack Center on Nonprofit and Pubic Sector Management in the Human Services.

CPSIA information can be obtained
at www.ICGtesting.com
Printed in the USA
LVHW050715100119
603330LV00008B/29/P